AITAREYA

With the Commentary of
ŚAṄKARĀCĀRYA

Translated by
SWĀMĪ GAMBHĪRĀNANDA

Advaita Ashrama
(Publication Department)
5 Dehi Entally Road
Kolkata 700 014

Published by
Swami Bodhasarananda
President, Advaita Ashrama
Mayavati, Champawat, Uttaranchal
from its Publication Department, Kolkata
Email: *mail@advaitaashrama.org*
Website: *www.advaitaashrama.org*

Fifth Impression, October 2006
2M2C

ISBN 81-85301-34-4

Printed in India at
Trio Process
Kolkata 700 014

AITAREYA UPANIṢAD

PUBLISHER'S NOTE TO THE FIRST EDITION

In 1957–58, we had published *Eight Upaniṣads*, in two volumes, the first comprising the Īśā, Kena, Kaṭha, and Taittirīya Upaniṣads, and the second containing the Aitareya, Muṇḍaka, Māṇḍukya with the Kārikā, and Praśna Upaniṣads, with the English translation of the texts and of Śaṅkarācārya's commentary on each of them. Beginning with the Aitareya Upaniṣad from the second volume, we now propose to publish, separately, each of these Upaniṣads with the English translation of the commentary on it, without any editing. The two-volume edition, *Eight Upaniṣads* will also continue to be published.

We hope the Upaniṣads, thus published, will better meet the growing interest in their study and in the famous commentary on them.

The Aitareya Upaniṣad is contained in the Ṛg-Veda, and forms a part of the Aitareya Āraṇyaka. The portion of the Āraṇyaka preceding the Upaniṣad deals with rituals for attainment of identity with Prāṇa, i.e. Saguṇa Brahman. The Upaniṣad itself, however, as Śaṅkarācārya argues and establishes in his commentary, holds out a distinct goal—realization of the identity of the individual soul with Nirguṇa Brahman, which is pure Consciousness.

The Upaniṣad teaches this goal by the method of assumption (*adhyāropa*) of names and forms, of phenomena as real, and its refutation (*apavāda*). The verses up to I. iii. 13 deal with *adhyāropa*, and then commence those dealing with *apavāda*, leading up the seeker to the true nature of Reality. The Upanisad concludes by proclaiming Brahman as Consciousness (प्रज्ञानं ब्रह्म) to be the basis of everything (प्रज्ञाने प्रतिष्ठितम्).

PUBLISHER

PUBLISHER'S NOTE TO THE SECOND EDITION

In this second edition of the *Aitareya Upaniṣad*, the translator himself has revised it thoroughly.

Mayavati
1 March 1988

PUBLISHER

KEY TO TRANSLITERATION AND PRONUNCIATION

		Sounds like
अ	a	o in s*o*n
आ	ā	a in m*a*ster
इ	i	i in *i*f
ई	ī	ee in f*ee*l
उ	u	u in f*u*ll
ऊ	ū	oo in b*oo*t
ऋ	ṛ	somewhat between r and ri
ए	e	a in ev*a*de
ऐ	ai	y in m*y*
ओ	o	o in *o*ver
औ	au	ow in n*ow*
क	k	k
ख	kh	ckh in blo*ckh*ead
ग	g	g (hard)
घ	gh	gh in log-*h*ut
ङ	ṅ	ng
च	c	ch (not k)
छ	ch	chh in cat*ch h*im
ज	j	j
झ	jh	dgeh in he*dgeh*og
ञ	ñ	n (somewhat)
ट	ṭ	t
ठ	ṭh	th in a*nt-h*ill

		Sounds like
ड	ḍ	d
ढ	ḍh	dh in go*dh*ood
ण	ṇ	n in u*n*der
त	t	French t
थ	th	th in *th*umb
द	d	th in *th*en
ध	dh	theh in brea*the h*ere
न	n	n
प	p	p
फ	ph	ph in loo*p-h*ole
ब	b	b
भ	bh	bh in a*bh*or
म	m	m
य	y	y
र	r	r
ल	l	l
व	v	in a*v*ert
श	ś	sh
ष	ṣ	sh in *sh*ow
स	s	s
ह	h	h
ं	ṁ	m in hu*m*
:	ḥ	half h in hu*h*!

LIST OF ABBREVIATIONS

A.G.	...	Ānanda Giri
Ai.Ā.	...	Aitareya Āraṇyaka
Bṛ.	...	Bṛhadāraṇyaka Upaniṣad
Ch.	...	Chāndogya Upaniṣad
G.	...	Bhagavad Gītā
Hari.	...	Harivaṁśa
Īś.	...	Īśā Upaniṣad
Jā.	...	Jābāla Upaniṣad
Kai.	...	Kaivalya Upaniṣad
Kau.	...	Kauṣītakī Upaniṣad
Ke.	...	Kena Upaniṣad
M.	...	Manu Saṁhitā
Mai.	...	Maitrāyaṇī Upaniṣad
Mu.	...	Muṇḍaka Upaniṣad
Np.	...	Nārada-Parivrājaka Upaniṣad
Pr.	...	Praśna Upaniṣad
Ṛ.	...	Ṛg-Veda
Śv.	...	Śvetāśvatara Upaniṣad
Tai.	...	Taittirīya Upaniṣad
Tai. S.	...	Taittirīya Saṁhitā

AITAREYA UPANIṢAD

ॐ वाङ् मे मनसि प्रतिष्ठिता मनो मे वाचि प्रतिष्ठित-
माविरावीर्म एधि वेदस्य म आणीस्थः श्रुतं मे मा प्रहासीरने-
नाधीतेनाहोरात्रान् संदधाम्यृतं वदिष्यामि सत्यं वदिष्यामि
तन्मामवतु तद्वक्तारमवत्ववतु मामवतु वक्तारमवतु वक्तारम्।

ॐ शान्तिः शान्तिः शान्तिः ॥

Om! May my speech be based on (i.e. accord with) the mind; may my mind be based on speech. O Self-effulgent One, reveal Thyself to me. May you both (speech and mind) be the carriers of the Veda to me. May not all that I have heard depart from me. I shall join together (i.e. obliterate the difference of) day and night through this study. I shall utter what is verbally true; I shall utter what is mentally true. May That (Brahman) protect me; may That protect the speaker (i.e. the teacher); may That protect me; may That protect the speaker, may That protect the speaker.

Om! Peace! Peace! Peace!

AITAREYA UPANIṢAD

PART I

CHAPTER I

Introduction: Earlier than this[1] was finished *karma*[2] along with the knowledge of (i.e. meditation on) the inferior Brahman (i.e. Hiranyagarbha). This highest result that is such and achievable through *karma*, associated with meditation, was concluded with the meditation on Uktha.[3] It was said, 'This Brahman that is Truth is called Prāna; this is the only Deity' (Kau. II. 2; Mai. VII. 7); 'All the gods are but manifestations of this Prāṇa'; 'Attaining identity with (the Deity, Brahmā, Immortality, that is) this Prāṇa, one becomes united with the gods.' Some people believe that the highest human goal consists in this merger in the Deity, that this is emancipation, that this is attainable by the means of a combination of meditation and *karma* as described, and that there is nothing higher than this. With a view to refuting them and enjoining the knowledge of the absolute Self, the subsequent text says,

[1] The Aitareya Upaniṣad forms the 4th, 5th and 6th chapters of the second Āraṇyaka of Aitareya Brāhmaṇa. The Upaniṣad is concerned only with knowledge of the Self, whereas the earlier portions deal with *karma*, associated with meditation.

[2] Rites, duties, etc.

[3] Uktha is Prāṇa (lit. Vital Force, i.e. Hiranyagarbha—cosmic power of knowledge and action); and meditation on it consists in thinking, 'I am that Uktha or Prāṇa.' Such deep concentration ensures identity with Prāṇa.

'In the beginning this was but the absolute Self alone', etc. (I. i. 1).

Objection: How is it, again, known that the subsequent text is meant for enjoining the knowledge of the absolute Self, unconnected with *karma*?

Answer: Since no other meaning can be deduced. Moreover, through such texts as 'He subjected Him[1] to hunger and thirst' (I. ii. 1) etc., it will be shown that the gods such as Fire, mentioned earlier, are included in the phenomenal world because of the defects of their hunger etc. All that is subject to hunger etc. is surely within the phenomenal world, whereas the supreme Brahman is mentioned in the Vedas as transcendental to hunger and the rest.

Objection: Even if it be thus conceded that the knowledge of the absolute Self is the means for emancipation, it does not follow that a non-performer of *karma* alone is qualified for this, since no such specification is heard of, there being no mention in this Upaniṣad of any non-performer of *karma* (i.e. a *sannyāsī*) belonging to a distinct order. Again, the knowledge of the Self is begun only after introducing the rite called Bṛhatī-sahasra. Therefore it is the performer of *karma* who is in fact entitled to this. Nor is the knowledge of the Self incompatible with *karma*, for the summing up (here) at the end conforms to what went earlier. Just as it was stated by the (earlier) *brāhmaṇa* (portion) that the Puruṣa[2] associated with *karma* and identified with the Sun, is the Self of all beings, mobile and

[1] Virāṭ, who is the gross manifestation of Hiraṇyagarbha.
[2] The conscious, all-pervasive Reality that dwells everywhere.

immobile,[1] and as it was confirmed by the *mantra* (portion) in such texts as, 'The Sun is the Self (of the universe, moving and motionless)' (Ṛ. I. cxv. 1), similarly (here), too, the start will be made with 'This one is (the inferior) Brahman; this is Indra' (III. i. 3), and the conclusion will be, 'All the creatures that there are, which move or do not move, are impelled by Consciousness' (III. i. 3). Similarly, too, in the Upaniṣad of the *saṁhitā* (portion) the Self will be spoken of as associated with *karma*, in the text, 'The followers of the Ṛg-Veda deliberate on this very Entity in the hymn called Bṛhatī-sahasra', etc. (Ai. Ā. III. ii. 3. 12), and the conclusion will be with, 'They speak of it alone as the Self in all beings', etc. Similarly, too, the identity of the One that is referred to in, 'That which the bodiless conscious Self', is spoken of in, 'One should know That as identical with Him that is in the sun'. Here, again, commencing with, 'Which is It that we worship as this Self?' (III. i. 1), the identity with Consciousness Itself will be shown in 'Consciousness is Brahman' (III. i. 3). Therefore the knowledge of the Self is not disconnected with *karma*.

Counter-objection: (On that supposition) the present text becomes useless because of tautology. How? The Self having been ascertained by the *brāhmaṇa* (portion) in, 'O Ṛṣi, I am indeed Prāṇa', and by the *mantra* (portion) in, 'The Sun is the Self' (Ṛ. I. cxv. 1), it is useless and tautological to ascertain It over again by the *brāhmaṇa*

[1] First His identity with the Sun is shown in, 'He indeed illumines this world—the One that shines as the Being (in the Sun)', and then He is shown as all-pervading in, 'Therefore they know Him as a hundred-rayed—the One that is that very Puruṣa', and, 'It is the vital force indeed that becomes all these' (Ch. V.i.15; VII.xv.4).

(i.e. the Upaniṣad portion) by raising the question, 'Which is It that we worship as this Self?' (III. i. 1) and then answering that 'all this is but the Self', and so on.

Opponent: Not so, for no fault of tautology is involved, inasmuch as this is meant to determine some special qualities of that very Self. How? Of that very Self, as connected with *karma*, it is sought to determine some special attributes such as (the power of) creation, protection, and dissolution of the world, or to present It as an object of meditation in Its unconditioned state. To explain the second alternative: From the fact that meditation on the Self (as such) was not enjoined in the context of *karma*, it might be inferred that the Self, which is (found) associated with *karma*, is not to be meditated upon apart from *karma*; therefore the purport of the (following) text, beginning with *'Ātmā'* etc., is that the unconditioned Self, too, is to be meditated on. Or since the Self is to be worshipped (both) as different and non-different (from oneself), the same Self that is subject to the idea of difference in a context of *karma* is again to be meditated on as non-different outside (that) *karma*. Thus there is no tautology. Moreover, according to the adherents of the Vājasaneya Section (of the Yajur-Veda) there are the statements, 'He who knows these two, *Vidyā* (knowledge) and *avidyā* (rites etc.), together, attains immortality through *vidyā* by crossing over death through *avidyā*' (Īś.11) and 'By doing *karma* indeed should one wish to live here for a hundred years' (Īś. 2). Not that mortals can have more than a hundred years as the fullest span of life, so as to be able to meditate on the Self after renouncing *karma* (after a hundred years). And it has been shown in the Aitareya Āraṇyaka, 'The span of a man's life comprises as many thousands of days.'[1] Now, the hundred years of life are packed with *karma*; and the *mantra*, 'By doing *karma* indeed . . .' has just been quoted. Similar are the texts, 'One should perform the Agnihotra sacrifices as long as one lives', 'One should perform the Darśa and Pūrṇamāsa (new moon and full moon) sacrifices as long as one lives', and others, as well as, 'Him they burn along with the sacrificial vessels.' Besides, there is the Vedic text speaking of the three debts.[2] As for the scriptural text dealing with monasticism etc., to wit, 'Knowing this very Self the Brāhmaṇas renounce, . . . and lead a mendicant life' (Bṛ. III. v. 1, IV. iv. 22), it is eulogistic, meant to praise the knowledge of the Self. Or it is meant for the disqualified ones (e.g. the blind, the lame, and others)[3].

Vedāntin: Not so, for when the supreme knowledge is achieved, there can be no idea of results, and so no action is possible. As for the statements that 'the knowledge of the Self comes to the man engaged in *karma*', that 'it is associated with *karma*', and so on, they are wrong. Action is inconceivable in one who has the knowledge of Brahman as his Self, comprised in the realization, 'I am the supreme Brahman in which all desires are fulfilled and which is above all the worldly shortcomings', and who has no idea of

[1] The Āraṇyaka first points out that the *śāstra* (hymn) called Bṛhatī-sahasra has got 36,000 letters in it, and then states that a man's life consists of as many days, that is, 100 years.

[2] 'The Brāhmaṇa, from his birth, is under three debts' (Tai. S. VI. iii. 10) — to the gods, manes, and sages.

[3] Who cannot undertake Vedic rites.

results because he feels no need for anything to be got for himself from actions done or to be done (by him).

Objection: Though he may not perceive any benefit therefrom, he still acts because of the (scriptural) injunction.

Answer: No, for he has realized the Self that is beyond the range of injunctions. It is seen in the world that one comes within the scope of injunction so long as one feels the need for acquiring some desirable thing or avoiding some undesirable thing for himself and seeks for a means thereof; but not is so the one who is of a contrary disposition and has realized the identity of the Self with Brahman that cannot be subjected to any injunction. If a man who has realized the identity of the Self and Brahman has still to bow down to injunctions, even though he is beyond all mandates, then there will remain none who is outside the pale of scriptural direction; and so all actions will become fit to be undertaken by all and sundry at all times. But that is undesirable. Nor can he be directed by anybody, for even the scriptures emanate from him. Not that anyone can himself be impelled by any sentence issuing out of his own wisdom. Nor is a well-informed master commanded by an ignorant servant.

Objection: The Vedas, being eternal, are independent, and hence have the mandatory power over all.

Answer: No, for the defect (of such an argument) has been already pointed out. Even on this assumption, the defect of every duty becoming fit to be indiscriminately undertaken at all times by all and sundry persists unavoidably.

Objection: That, too, is enjoined by the scriptures. (To explain:) As performance of duties is prescribed by scriptures, so is the knowledge of the Self prescribed for that man of *karma* by the scriptures themselves.

Answer: No, for it is impossible that the scriptures should be prescribing contradictory things. Just as heat and cold cannot both be averred of fire, so it is not possible to instruct, for the same person, association with as well as dissociation from present and future actions. Nor are the desires to attain the delectable and avoid the detestable for oneself creations of the scriptures, for all beings are seen to have them. Had these two been the products of the scriptures, they would not have been found in the cowherds and others, who are ignorant of scriptures. The scriptures have to instruct about those things only that are not self-evident. That being so, if the scriptures have produced the knowledge of the Self, opposed to (ideas of) duties that have been accomplished or are yet to be accomplished, how can they again produce the sense of duty that runs counter to it, like coldness in fire or darkness in the sun?

Objection: The scriptures certainly do not generate such a knowledge.

Answer: No, since the conclusion is made thus: 'One should know thus: "He is my Self"' (Kau. III. 9), 'Consciousness is Brahman' (III. i. 3). And sentences such as, 'It knew only Itself (as "I am Brahman"; therefore It became all)' (Bṛ. I. iv. 10), 'Thou art That' (Ch. VI. viii-xvi), bear on the same idea. And since the knowledge of the identity of the Self and Brahman, once it has emerged, is never sublated, its origination cannot be denied or pronounced erroneous.

Objection: With regard to renunciation, too, there is an equal absence of need, in accordance with the Smṛti, '(He has no object in this world to gain by doing action), nor by non-performance' (G. III. 18). Those who say that after realizing Brahman one must resort to renunciation are equally open to the same charge of 'absence of need'.

Answer: No, since renunciation consists in mere cessation from activity. The feeling of want follows from ignorance and is not inherent in any object, for this fact (of feeling of want towards an object) is in evidence in all beings[1]. Moreover, it is noticed that one acts through speech, mind, and body when one is impelled by thirst for desired results; and by the text beginning with, 'He desired, "Let me have a wife"' (Bṛ. I. iv. 17), and by the text, 'Both these are but desires (for ends and means)' (Bṛ. III. v. 1, IV. iv. 22), of the Vājasaneya Brāhmaṇa, it has been emphatically asserted that sons, wealth, etc., that constitute the fivefold *karma*[2] are comprised within desire. Since the activities of speech, mind, and body with regard to the (fivefold) Vedic rituals, arising from such defects as ignorance, desire, etc., cannot belong to a man of realization because of his freedom from the defects like ignorance etc., his renunciation consists in the mere absence of activity;

[1] Even in people who are ignorant of the nature of things. This is according to the reading, '*taddarśanāt*'. Ānanda Giri prefers '*tadadarśanāt*—is not in evidence'. If the feeling inhered in the object, all should have felt it similarly and for ever. The reaction being different, the feeling is subjective.

[2] The metre called Paṅkti has five letters in each foot; and in sacrifices the five factors—wife, son, divine wealth (meditation), human wealth, and rites—get conjoined. Hence sacrifices are *pāṅkta*, constituted by five factors.

and it is not a positive something to be accomplished like sacrifice etc. And that being a natural accomplishment of a man of illumination, no need is to be sought for it. No such question can be raised as to the need because of which a person, who was (once) enveloped in darkness, does not fall into a pit, swamp, or brambles after the dawn of light.

Objection: Then it comes to this that renunciation follows as a matter of course and is not fit to be enjoined. Therefore, if the supreme knowledge of Brahman dawns in domestic life, the inactive[1] man may continue in that state, and there need be no moving away from it.

Answer: No, since domestic life is induced by desire, for it has been clearly declared, 'This much indeed is desire'[2] (Br. I. iv. 17), 'Both these[3] are indeed desires' (Br. III. v. 1, IV. iv. 22). Renunciation is defined as the mere absence of well-established relationship with sons etc. arising from desire, and not as the mere moving away from that domestic life. And so the inactive man of realization cannot continue in the domestic life itself.[4] Hereby it is established that for an illumined soul there can be no acceptance of such duties as the service of the Guru, or (practice of) austerities.

Against this argument, some householders, shy of begging

[1] One who does not engage anymore in scriptural rituals etc.

[2] The first part of the sentence is: 'He desired, "Let me have a wife, so that I may be born (as a child). And let me have wealth, so that I may perform rites"'.

[3] Hankering for ends and means.

[4] He cannot consider himself a householder, nor can he deliberately put on the householder's garb or accept the latter's duties.

alms and afraid of ridicule, advance the following rejoinder, thereby making a show of their intellectual acumen:

Inasmuch as a mendicant, desirous merely of maintaining his body, is seen to subject himself to regulations about begging, there can be continuance in the domestic life even for that householder who has become freed from both kinds of desires with regard to ends and means, but who has to depend on mere food and raiment for the maintenance of the body.

Answer: Not so, for this has already been refuted by saying that the constant habit of resorting to any particular house of one's own is prompted by desire. When there is no clinging to any particular house of one's own, there follows begging alone, as a matter of course, in the case of one who has no special inclination for turning to his own and who seeks for food and raiment under the mere impulsion of maintaining the body.

Objection: Just as (for a *sannyāsī*) there are regulations with regard to engagement in begging for the sake of maintaining the body, as also with regard to personal cleanliness etc., so in the case of the householder, who has become illumined and free from desire, there may be regular engagement in obligatory duties — for the sake of avoiding evil — in pursuance of the injuction implied in the Vedic text enjoining *karma* for the whole life.

Answer: This has already been refuted by pointing out that the illumined soul is outside the range of injunction; besides, he cannot be impelled.

Objection: The injunction about obligatory duties contained in, 'One should perform the Agnihotra sacrifice for life', becomes meaningless thereby.

Answer: No, because it retains its meaningfulness with regard to the ignorant man. As for the regulation about the activities of the mendicant engaged in the mere support of the body, that regulation does not generate any action. Just as no fresh motive is in evidence in the matter of quenching thirst (*pari passu*) for a man engaged in sipping water from the palm of the hand as a ceremonial act, similarly (in the matter of rules for begging) no other impulse is in evidence (apart from assuaging hunger).[1] It cannot be argued on similar grounds that in the case of Agnihotra, too, the activities are derived naturally and are regulated accordingly.[2]

Objection: Restriction of even spontaneous activity is uncalled for when it serves no purpose.

Answer: No, since that restriction follows naturally out of past tendencies, and an overriding of them involves great effort.[3] From the fact that a fresh injunction of

[1] Following the injunction about sipping, a man sips water and the thirst is assuaged *pari passu*; but the latter fact is not the motive for the sipping. Similarly, a man engages naturally in begging food for life, and consequent on that there occur some rules; but these rules cannot lead to a supposition of some fresh motive for the begging.

[2] For these activities are not spontaneous, but follow from a desire for heaven etc.

[3] Life can be maintained by begging for alms, whether according to rules or not. But before the rise of knowledge, the mendicant had followed good rules as a spiritual discipline, and the habit persists even after illumination. The path of least resistance lies in following the habit and not in counteracting it.

renunciation, despite its emergence as a matter of course (in the case of a man of illumination), is met with,[1] it becomes evident that it is obligatory for the man of illumination. And monasticism is obligatory even for the unillumined soul that hankers after emancipation. With regard to this matter the sentence, 'Therefore he who knows thus becomes self-controlled, calm,' etc. (Bṛ. IV. iv. 23) can be cited as authoritative. Besides, such means for the realization of the Self as physical and mental control etc., are incompatible with other stages of life. And it is known from the Śvetāśvatara Upaniṣad, 'To those (monks) who are above the (four) stages of life he spoke well of that supremely holy Reality that is sought after by seers of Truth' (VI. 21). And in the Kaivalya Upaniṣad (2) there occurs this text, 'Some attained immortality not by *karma*, not by progeny, not by wealth, but by renunciation.'[2] And the Smṛti says, 'After attaining knowledge, one should have recourse to inactivity', and 'He should continue in that order of life (*sannyāsa*) which is conducive to the attainment of Brahman.' Moreover, the practice of such disciplines as for enlightenment, continence, in their fullness is possible only for those who are above the four stages of life, whereas it is impossible in domestic life. Not that an incomplete means can fulfil any objective (e.g. the realization of the Self). As for the kind of realization to which the *karmas* pertaining to the householder's life can lead, their highest result has been summed up as merger

[1] In Bṛ. III. v. I. etc.—'Knowing this very Self, the Brāhmaṇas renounce . . . and lead a mendicant life.'

[2] The idea is that the few who ever realized, did so through renunciation.

in the Deity (Hiraṇyagarbha), and that is within the worldly state itself. If the knowledge of the Self were possible for people engrossed only in *karma*, the conclusion there would not have been made with a result, (viz merger in the Deity), which is within the worldly state.

Objection: That is only the product of some subsidiary factor (associated with the higher knowledge).[1]

Answer: No, for the knowledge of the Self relates to the Reality which is the Self, and which is entirely opposed to it (viz the subsidiary). The means to the attainment of immortality is the knowledge of the Self which is the supreme Reality beyond all names, forms, and actions. If that knowledge remains associated with some secondary result (within the world), it cannot pertain to the Reality that is the Self from which are ruled out all distinctions. And that is undesirable, for in the text of the Vājasaneya Brāhmaṇa, beginning with 'Where everything becomes his Self' (Bṛ. II. iv. 14), all empirical dealings, involving actions, auxiliaries, and fruits have been denied for the illumined soul; and by saying, 'Where there is an appearance of duality' (Bṛ. IV. iv. 14), the worldly state comprised of actions, auxiliaries, and fruits has been shown in the case of the unillumined soul who is the opposite of the former. Similarly, here, too, the text thinks, 'I shall speak of that absolute knowledge of the all-pervasive Reality that leads to immortality after I have dealt with the fruit that consists in the identity with the Deity, exists within the worldly state, and is constituted by things subject to hunger etc.'

[1] E.g. the knowledge of Fire and other deities associated with the realization of the Self.

For the unenlightened man, again, and not the enlightened one, do the three debts act as impediments in the way to his attaining the worlds of men, manes, and gods, as it is established by the Vedic text, 'That world of men is to be conquered through the son alone' etc.[1] (Bṛ. I. v. 16), which determines the means for the attainment of the three worlds. And for the man of illumination craving for the world of the Self, the absence of impediment from debts is shown by 'What shall we achieve through children' etc. (Bṛ. IV. iv. 22). So also there are the texts of the Kauṣītakī branch, 'So the ancient seers, the Kāvaṣeyas, who had realized It said, ("Why should we study the Vedas?")' (Kau. II. 5) and 'The ancient illumined souls who knew It, did not perform the Agnihotra sacrifice' (*ibid*).

Objection: For the unillumined soul, then, there can be no monasticism before he clears the (three) debts.

Answer: Not so, because one does not become indebted before entering the householder's life. If one can become indebted irrespective of his obligation thereto, then all may as well become so, which (conclusion) will lead to undesirable consequences. In accordance with the text, 'From the domestic life he should resort to that of the forest-dweller (recluse), and then embrace monasticism; alternatively, one may embrace monasticism from the stage of the celibate, or the householder, or the recluse' (Jā. 4), even for one who has embraced the householder's life, monasticism is desirable as a disciplinary means for the realization of the Self. The Vedic texts speaking of per-

[1] '. . . the world of manes through rites; and the world of the gods through meditation.'

formance of rites throughout life find their scope among the unenlightened souls who do not long for freedom. In (some recensions of) the Chāndogya, too, it is found that for some people it is enjoined that the Agnihotra sacrifice can be given up after performing it for twelve nights. As for the view that monasticism is meant for those who are disqualified (from performing *karma*), it is unsound, since with regard to them (the monks) an independent injunction occurs in, 'He whose fire has been extinguished or who has not lighted it up (shall renounce the day he becomes desireless)' (Np. III. 77). Moreover, it is a well-known fact that all the Smṛtis, in a general way, enjoin option with regard to, as well as adoption (in succession) of, all the stages of life. As for the argument, 'Inasmuch as renunciation ensues spontaneously in the case of the illumined soul, it is beyond the purview of the scriptures, and therefore it makes little difference as to whether he continues in domestic life or repairs to the forest', it is unsound, for absolute renunciation being a spontaneous result, there can be no continuance in any other order. We pointed out that involvement in any other stage of life is a result of the action of desire, and that renunciation consists merely in the absence of this. As for unchecked behaviour in the case of the illumined soul, it is entirely out of place, it being found among the extremely ignorant. Moreover, seeing that even scriptural duties are known to be inapplicable in the case of the knower of the Self, they being too burdensome, can he have unrestrained behaviour that arises from extreme non-discrimination? Not that a thing perceived under lunacy or through eyes affected by the Timira disease, continues to be exactly so when the disease is cured, that vision being contingent on lunacy or Timira.

Accordingly, it is proved that for the knower of the Self there can be neither wantonness nor engagement in any other duty apart from renunciation.

As for the text, 'He who knows these two, *vidyā* and *avidyā*, together' (Īś. 11), it does not convey the idea that ignorance, too, persists along with enlightenment for the man of knowledge. What is the meaning then? It is meant to imply that they cannot cohere in the same person at the same time, as for instance the ideas of silver and nacre cannot cohere in a person with regard to the same mother of pearl. For it is said in the Kaṭha Upaniṣad, 'That which is known as *vidyā* (knowledge) and that which is known as *avidyā* (rites, duties, etc.) are widely contradictory, and they follow divergent courses' (I. ii. 4). Hence there is no possibility of the continuance of ignorance when knowledge dawns. From such Vedic texts as 'Crave to know Brahman through concentration' (Tai. III. ii.), it follows that concentration etc. that are conducive to the rise of knowledge, as well as activities like service of the teacher, are called *avidyā* (nescience), since they are the products of nescience. Producing *vidyā* (knowledge) through them, one transcends death that is the same as desire. Then the passionless man renounces all desires and achieves immortality through the knowledge of Brahman. In order to reveal this idea the (Īśā) Upaniṣad says, 'Crossing over death through *avidyā*, one attains immortality through *vidyā*' (11). As for the view that the entire span of a man's life is packed with *karma* according to the text, 'By doing *karma* indeed should one wish to live here for a hundred years' (Īś. 2), that has been dismissed as relating to the ignorant, for otherwise it would be untenable. And the argument was advanced that what follows (in the present Upaniṣad) is in line with what preceded it, and therefore the knowledge of the Self is not opposed to *karma*. This view was disposed of by relating the two standpoints to the conditioned and the unconditioned Self, and this will be shown by us in the succeeding explanation. Therefore the following text is commenced in order to reveal the knowledge of the oneness of the Self and the absolute, actionless Brahman:

ॐ आत्मा वा इदमेक एवाग्र आसीत्। नान्यत् किंचन मिषत्। स ईक्षत लोकान्नु सृजा इति ॥१॥

1. *Om*! In the beginning this was but the absolute Self alone. There was nothing else whatsoever that winked. It thought, 'Let Me create the worlds.'

Ātmā vai, the absolute[1] Self. The word *ātmā*, Self, is derived in the sense of comprehending, engulfing, or pervading, and by it is signified one that is the highest, omniscient, omnipotent, and devoid of all such worldly attributes as hunger; by nature eternal, pure, conscious, and free; birthless, undecaying, immortal, deathless, fearless, and without a second. *Idam*, this—all that has been referred to as this world, diversified through the differences of name, form, and action; *āsīt*, was; *agre*, in the beginning, before the creation of this world; *ātmā ekaḥ eva*, but the one Self. *Objection*: Has It ceased to be the same one entity?

[1] *Vai* is used to present the absolute by way of ruling out the conditioned.

Answer: No.

Objection: Why is it then said, 'It was'?

Answer: Though even now that very same single entity endures, still there is some distinction. The distinction is this: The universe in which the differences of name and form were not manifest before creation, which was then one with the Self, and which was denotable by the single word and idea 'Self', has now become denotable by many words and concepts as well as by the single word and concept 'Self', because of its diversification through the multiplicity of names and forms. Foam is denoted by the single word and concept 'water', before the manifestation of names and forms distinct from water; but when that foam becomes manifested as (an entity) distinct from water, owing to the difference of name and form, then the very same foam becomes denotable by many words and concepts, viz foam and water, as well as by only one word and one concept, viz water. The same is the case here.

Na anyat kiṁcana, there was nothing else whatsoever; *miṣat*, winking, that was active or tractive. Unlike the Pradhāna of the Sāṁkhyas, which is an independent entity and not of the same class as the selves, and unlike the atoms of the followers of Kaṇāda, there remained here nothing whatsoever apart from the Self. What (existed) then? The Self alone existed. This is the idea. *Saḥ*, that Self; being naturally omniscient, *īkṣata*, thought; even though It was but one.

Objection: Since the Self was devoid of body and senses, how could It think before creation?

Answer: This is no fault, because of Its nature of omniscience, in support of which fact is the *mantra* text, 'Without hands and feet He goes and grasps' etc. (Śv. III. 19). With what motive (did He think)? The answer is: *sṛjai*, let Me create; *lokān*, the worlds—(viz) *ambhas* etc., which are the places for the enjoyment of the fruits of work done by creatures.

Having visualized, i.e. deliberated, thus,

स इमाँल्लोकानसृजत। अम्भो मरीचीर्मरमापोऽदोऽम्भः परेण दिवं द्यौः प्रतिष्ठाऽन्तरिक्षं मरीचयः पृथिवी मरो या अधस्तात्ता आपः ॥२॥

2. He created these worlds, viz *ambhas, marīci, mara, āpaḥ*. That which is beyond heaven is *ambhas*. Heaven is its support. The sky is *marīci*. The earth is *mara*. The worlds that are below are the *āpaḥ*.

Sah, that Self; *asṛjata*, created; *imān lokān*, these worlds; just as in the world an intelligent architect or others think, 'I shall construct a palace etc. according to this plan', and build up the palace etc. after that deliberation.

Objection: It is logical that architects and others, possessed of materials, should raise up palaces etc. But how can the Self, devoid of materials, create the worlds?

Answer: This is nothing wrong. Name and form—which remain identified with the Self in their unmanifested state just like the (undiversified) foam with water, and are hence denotable by the word 'Self'—can become the material cause of the universe, as water becomes that of the manifested foam. Therefore there is nothing incongruous in saying that the omniscient Being creates the universe by virtue of Its oneness with the materials—viz name and form—which are identified with Itself. Or the more reasonable position is this: Just as an intelligent juggler, who has no material, transforms himself, as it were, into a second self ascending into space, similarly the omniscient and omnipotent Deity, who is a supreme magician, creates Himself as another in the form of the universe. On this view, the schools that hold such beliefs as the unreality of both cause and effect have no legs to stand on and are totally demolished.

Which are the worlds that He created? They are being enumerated: *Ambhas, marīcīḥ, maram, āpaḥ*. Starting with space, he created in due order the cosmic egg, and then created the worlds—*ambhas* etc. As for these, the Upaniṣad itself explains the words *ambhas* etc. *Adaḥ*, that one—the world that is there; *pareṇa divam*, beyond heaven; is *ambhas*, is denoted by the word *ambhas*. It is called *ambhas* because it holds *ambhas*, water (cloud). Of that world, viz *ambhas*, *dyauḥ pratiṣṭhā*, heaven is the support. *Antarikṣam*, the sky, which is there below heaven, is the (world called) *marīci* (lit. sunrays). Though this (last) world is one, it is used in the plural number as *marīcīḥ* (or rather *marīcayaḥ*) because of the diversity of the space covered by it. Or it is so used because of its association with the *marīcayaḥ*, rays (of the sun). *Pṛthivī*, the earth, is *maraḥ* since beings die (*mriyante*) on it. *Yāḥ adhastāt*, the worlds that are below—below the earth; *tāḥ*, they (are); *āpaḥ*, called *āpaḥ*, (lit. water) the word being derived (from the root *āp*) in the sense of being *attained*[1]. Though the worlds are constituted by the five elements, still, because of the predominance of water (etc. in them), they are referred to, by the synonyms of water (etc.) as *ambhas*, *marīcīḥ*, *maram*, *āpaḥ*.

स ईक्षतेमे नु लोका लोकपालान्नु सृजा इति। सोऽद्भ्य एव पुरुषं समुद्धृत्यामूर्छयत् ॥३॥

3. He thought, 'These then are the worlds. Let Me create the protectors of the worlds.' Having gathered up a (lump of the) human form from the water itself, He gave shape to it.

Having created the four worlds that provide support for the fruits of action as well as the materials for those fruits[2] of all creatures, *saḥ*, He, God; *īkṣata*, deliberated; again *iti*, thus: '*Ime nu lokāḥ*, these then are the worlds, viz *ambhas* etc., created by Me, which will perish if they are devoid of protectors. Accordingly, for their preservation, *nu sṛjai*, let Me create; *lokapālān*, the protectors of the worlds.' After deliberating thus, *saḥ*, He; *samuddhṛtya*, having gathered up; *puruṣam*, a human form, possessed of head, hands, etc.; *adbhyaḥ*, from the water, itself—from the five elements in which water predominated, and from which He had created (the worlds, viz) *ambhas* etc.—just as a potter gathers up a lump of clay from the earth; *amūrchayat*, (He) gave shape to it—that is to say, fashioned it by endowing it with limbs.[3]

[1] *Attained* by the denizens of the nether worlds.
[2] And the accessories for achieving those fruits.
[3] He created Virāṭ.

तमभ्यतपत्तस्याभितप्तस्य मुखं निरभिद्यत यथाऽण्डम् । मुखाद्वाग्वाचोऽग्निर्नासिके निरभिद्येतां नासिकाभ्यां प्राणः प्राणाद्वायुरक्षिणी निरभिद्येतामक्षिभ्यां चक्षुश्चक्षुष आदित्यः कर्णौ निरभिद्येतां कर्णाभ्यां श्रोत्रं श्रोत्राद्दिशस्त्वङ्निरभिद्यत त्वचो लोमानि लोमभ्य ओषधिवनस्पतयो हृदयं निरभिद्यत हृदयान्मनो मनसश्चन्द्रमा नाभिर्निरभिद्यत नाभ्या अपानोऽपानान्मृत्युः शिश्नं निरभिद्यत शिश्नाद्रेतो रेतस आपः ॥४॥

इत्यैतरेयोपनिषदि प्रथमाध्याये प्रथमः खण्डः ॥

4. He deliberated with regard to Him (i.e. Virāṭ of the human form). As He (i.e. Virāṭ) was being deliberated on, His (i.e. Varāṭ's) mouth parted, just as an egg does. From the mouth emerged speech; from speech came Fire. The nostrils parted; from the nostrils came out the sense of smell; from the sense of smell came Vāyu (Air). The two eyes parted; from the eyes emerged the sense of sight; from the sense of sight came the Sun. The two ears parted; from the ears came the sense of hearing; from the sense of hearing came the Directions. The skin emerged; from the skin came out hair (i.e. the sense of touch associated with hair); from the sense of touch came the Herbs and Trees. The heart took shape; from the heart issued the internal organ (mind); from the internal organ came the Moon. The navel parted; from the navel came out the organ of ejection; from the organ of ejection issued Death. The seat of the procreative organ parted; from that came the pro-

creative organ; from the procreative organ came out Water.[1]

Tam, with regard to Him, (Virāṭ of) that human form; He *abhyatapat*, undertook *tapas* (lit. austerity), i.e. He deliberated over, or resolved about, Him; for a Vedic text says, 'Whose *tapas* is constituted by knowledge' (Mu. I. i. 9). *Tasya abhitaptasya*, of that (Virāṭ), of the lump (that was Virāṭ's body), when subjected to the *tapas* or resolution of God; *mukham nirabhidyata*, the mouth parted—a hole in the shape of the mouth emerged, just as the bird's egg bursts. *Mukhāt*, from that mouth which had parted; was brought into existence *vāk*, the organ of speech; *vācaḥ*, from that *vāk*; was produced *agniḥ*, Fire, (the deity) that presides over *vāk* and is a regional protector. Similarly *nāsike nirabhidyetām*, the nostrils parted; *nāsikābhyām prāṇaḥ*, from the nostrils emerged the sense of smell[2]; *prāṇāt vāyuḥ*, from the sense of smell was formed Vāyu, Air. Thus, in all cases, the seat of the organs, the organs, and the deity—these three emerged in succession. *Akṣiṇī*, the two eyes; *karṇau*, the two orifices of the ears; *tvak*, skin—(all these which are the seats of the organs), (and) *hṛdayam*, heart (which is the) seat of the internal organ; *manaḥ*, mind, the internal organ; *nābhiḥ*, the navel (i.e. the root of the anus)[3], which is the focal point of the vital forces. The organ of ejection (seated at the anus) is called *apānaḥ*, because of its association with Apāna (the vital force that moves down). From that originated its presiding

[1] Thus originated the presiding deities of the organs from the limbs of Virāṭ.

[2] The sense of smell together with Prāṇa.

[3] See A.G.

deity *mṛtyuḥ*, Death. As in the other cases, so *śiśnam*, the seat of the organ of generation was formed. Its organ is *retas*, semen—the organ meant for discharging semen being called semen from the fact of its association with semen. From semen (i.e. the procreative organ) emerged (its deity) *āpaḥ*, Water.

CHAPTER II

ता एता देवताः सृष्टा अस्मिन्महत्यर्णवे प्रापतन्। तमशनायापिपासाभ्यामन्ववार्जत्। ता एनमब्रुवन्नायतनं नः प्रजानीहि यस्मिन् प्रतिष्ठिता अन्नमदामेति ॥१॥

1. These deities, that had been created, fell into this vast ocean. He subjected Him (i.e. Virāṭ) to hunger and thirst. They said to Him (i.e. to the Creator), 'Provide an abode for us, staying where we can eat food.'

Tāḥ etāḥ devatāḥ, these deities—Fire and others; *sṛṣṭāḥ*, that had been created as the rulers of the regions, by God after deliberation; (fell) *asmin*, into this; *mahati arṇave*, vast ocean—the world which is like a vast ocean, that is filled with the water of sorrow arising from ignorance, desire, and action; that is infested with huge sea-animals in the form of acute disease, and age, and death; that has no beginning, end, and limit, and provides no resting place; that affords only momentary respite through the little joys arising from the contact of senses and objects; that is full of the high waves in the shape of hundreds of evils, stirred up by the gale of hankering for the objects of the five senses; that resounds with the noise of cries and shrieks of 'alas! alas!' etc., issuing from the beings condemned to various hells like Mahāraurava; that has the raft of knowledge—which is furnished with such provisions for the way as truth, simplicity, charity, compassion, non-injury, control of inner and outer organs, fortitude, etc. that are the embellishments of the heart, and which has good company and renunciation of everything as its course—and that has emancipation as its shore. Into this vast ocean, *prāpatan*, (they) fell. Hence, the idea sought to be imparted here is that even the attainment of the state of merger in the deities, viz Fire and others, which was explained (earlier), and which is the result of the combined practice of meditation and *karma*—(even this) is not adequate for the removal of the sorrows of the world. Since this is so, therefore, after having grasped this fact, one should, for the eradication of all the worldly miseries, realize the supreme Brahman as the Self of one's own as also of all beings—the Self which is possessed of the characteristics to be mentioned hereafter, and which has been introduced as the source of the origination, continuance, and dissolution of the universe. Therefore in accordance with the Vedic text, 'There is no other path for reaching there' (Śv. III. 8, VI. 15), it follows that, 'This that is the knowledge of the oneness of Brahman and the Self, is the path, this is the *karma*, this is Brahman, this is truth' (Ai. Ā. II. i. 1).

(He, the Creator) *anvavārjat*, suffused, i.e. endowed; *tam*, Him—who was the source of the organs, their seats, and their deities, the Being (i.e. Virāṭ) who was the first begotten and the Self in the form of a lump; *aśanāyā*-

pipāsābhyām, with hunger and thirst. Since He (the first begotten), the source of all, was afflicted with the defects of hunger etc. His products, the deities are also subject to hunger etc. Thereafter, *tāḥ*, those (deities); being afflicted with hunger and thirst; *abruvan*, said; *iti*, this; *enam*, to Him, to the grandsire, to the Creator (of the body of Virāṭ); '*Prajānīhi*, provide; *naḥ*, for us; *āyatanam*, an abode; *pratiṣṭhitāḥ yasmin*, staying where—and becoming able; *annam adāma*, we can eat food.'

ताभ्यो गामानयत्ता अब्रुवन्न वै नोऽयमलमिति। ताभ्यो-ऽश्वमानयत्ता अब्रुवन्न वै नोऽयमलमिति ॥२॥

2. For them He (i.e. God) brought a cow. They said, 'This one is certainly not adequate for us.' For them He brought a horse. They said, 'This one is certainly not adequate for us.'

God, having been told so, *tābhyaḥ*, for them, for the deities; *ānayat gām*, brought a cow; having gathered up a lump of the size of a cow from that very water, just as before, and having fashioned it, He showed it (to them). *Tāḥ*, they, on their part, having seen the bovine form; *abruvan*, said; '*Ayam*, this one—this lump; *na vai*, is certainly not; *alam*, adequate; *naḥ*, for us—not fit to serve as a seat while eating food; that is to say, it is not sufficient so far as eating is concerned.' The cow having been rejected, He *ānayat*, brought; *aśvam*, a horse; *tābhyaḥ*, for them. *Tāḥ*, they; *abruvan*, said; *iti*, this—just as before; '*Ayam na vai alam naḥ*, this is certainly not enough for us.'

ताभ्यः पुरुषमानयत्ता अब्रुवन् सुकृतं बतेति पुरुषो वाव सुकृतम्। ता अब्रवीद्यथायतनं प्रविशतेति ॥३॥

3. For them He brought a man. They said, 'This one is well formed: man indeed is a creation of God Himself.' To them He said, 'Enter into your respective abodes.'

When all else had been rejected, *tābhyaḥ*, for them; *ānayat*, (He) brought; *puruṣam*, a man, their progenitor[1]. Having seen that man, who was their source, they became free from misery, and *tāḥ*, they; *abruvan*, said; *iti*, this; 'This abode is *sukṛtam bata*, well created, to be sure.' As a result *puruṣaḥ vāva*, man is indeed; *sukṛtam*, virtue itself—he having become the source of all virtuous deeds.[2] Or, he is called *sukṛta*, (lit.) created by oneself, because God created man by Himself, through His own Māyā.[3] God thought that this abode was liked by them, since all beings love the source (from which they spring); and so He *abravīt*, said; *tāḥ*, to them, to the deities; *iti*, this; '*Praviśata*, enter; *yathāyatanam*, into the respective abode—into the dwelling that suits each for such activities as speaking etc.'

अग्निर्वाग्भूत्वा मुखं प्राविशद्वायुः प्राणो भूत्वा नासिके प्राविशदादित्यश्चक्षुर्भूत्वाऽक्षिणी प्राविशद्दिशः श्रोत्रं भूत्वा कर्णौ प्राविशन्नोषधिवनस्पतयो लोमानि भूत्वा त्वचं प्राविशं-श्चन्द्रमा मनो भूत्वा हृदयं प्राविशन्मृत्युरपानो भूत्वा नाभिं प्राविशदापो रेतो भूत्वा शिश्नं प्राविशन् ॥४॥

1 Who conformed in features to Virāṭ, their origin.

2 Since they pronounced man as *sukṛta*, therefore man acts virtuously even today.

3 Man was a good product, since God created him independently of servants and accessories. *Sukṛta* is thus explained in three senses—good product, virtue, created by oneself (*sva*).

4. Fire entered into the mouth taking the form of the organ of speech; Air entered into the nostrils assuming the form of the sense of smell; the Sun entered into the eyes as the sense of sight; the Directions entered into the ears by becoming the sense of hearing; the Herbs and Trees entered into the skin in the form of hair (i.e. the sense of touch); the Moon entered into the heart in the shape of the mind; Death entered into the navel in the form of Apāna (i.e. the vital force that presses down); Water entered into the limb of generation in the form of semen (i.e. the organ of procreation).

Just as the commander and others of armies etc. (enter) into a city (at the bidding of the king), so having got the permission of God with the words, 'Let this be so', *agniḥ*, Fire, the deity that identifies himself with the organ of speech; *bhūtvā*, becoming; *vāk*, speech itself; *prāviśat*, entered; *mukham*, into the mouth, which was his source. Similarly are the rest to be explained. *Vāyuḥ*, Air, entered *nāsike*, into the nostrils. *Ādityaḥ*, the Sun; *akṣiṇī*, into the eyes; *diśaḥ*, the Directions; *karṇau*, into the ears; *oṣadhi-vanaspatayaḥ*, the Herbs and Trees; *tvacam*, into the skin; *candramāḥ*, the Moon; *hṛdayam*, into the heart; *mṛtyuḥ*, Death; *nābhim*, into the navel (i.e. the root of the anus); *āpaḥ*, Water; *śiśnam*, into the generative organ.

तमशनायापिपासे अब्रूतामावाभ्यामभिप्रजानीहीति ते अब्रवीदेतास्वेव वां देवतास्वाभजाम्येतासु भागिन्यौ करोमीति। तस्माद्यस्यै कस्यै च देवतायै हविर्गृह्यते भागिन्यावेवास्यामशनायापिपासे भवतः ॥५॥

इत्यैतरेयोपनिषदि प्रथमाध्याये द्वितीयः खण्डः ॥

5. To Him Hunger and Thirst said, 'Provide for us (some abode).' To them He said, 'I provide your livelihood among these very gods; I make you share in their portions.' Therefore when oblation is taken up (for being offered) for any deity whichsoever, Hunger and Thirst become verily sharers with that deity.

When the gods had thus found their abodes, *aśanāyā-pipāse*, Hunger and Thirst, being without abodes; *abrūtām*, said, to that God; '*Āvābhyām*, for us; *abhiprajānīhi*, think of, i.e. provide; some abode.' He, God, having been told thus, *abravīt*, said; *te*, to those two—to Hunger and Thirst: 'Since you are but feelings, you cannot possibly eat food without being supported by some conscious being. Therefore *etāsu eva*, among these beings themselves; *devatāsu*, among the deities, viz Fire etc.—in the corporeal context, as also in the divine context; *ābhajāmi vām*, I favour you by apportioning your livelihood. *Karomi*, I make you; *bhāginyau*, sharers; *etāsu*, among these gods. Whatever allotment, consisting of oblation etc., is assigned to any deity, I make you share in that very portion.' Since God ordained thus in the beginning of creation, *tasmāt*, therefore; even today; *yasyai kasyai ca devatāyai*, for whichsoever deity; *haviḥ*, an oblation—such as porridge, cake, etc.; *gṛhyate*, is taken up; *aśanāyā-pipāse*, Hunger and Thirst; *bhāginyau eva bhavataḥ*, become sharers indeed; *asyām*, with that deity.

CHAPTER III

स ईक्षतेमे नु लोकाश्च लोकपालाश्चन्नमेभ्यः सृजा इति ॥१॥

1. He thought, 'This, then, are the senses and the deities of the senses. Let Me create food for them.'

Saḥ, He, God; *īkṣata*, thought thus. How? '*Ime nu*, these then are; *lokāḥ ca lokapālāḥ ca*, the senses and their deities — which have been created by Me and dowered with hunger and thirst; therefore these cannot subsist without food. Accordingly, *sṛjai* (which is the same as *sṛje*), let Me create; *annam*, food; *ebhyaḥ*, for these — the deities of the senses.' Thus is seen in the world the independence of lordly persons with regard to extending favour or disfavour to their own people. Therefore the supreme Lord, too, has independence in the matter of favouring or disfavouring all, since He is the Lord of all.

सोऽपोऽभ्यतपत्ताभ्योऽभितप्ताभ्यो मूर्तिरजायत। या वै सा मूर्तिरजायतान्नं वै तत् ॥२॥

2. He deliberated with regard to the water. From the water, thus brooded over, evolved a form. The form that emerged was verily food.

Saḥ, He, God; being desirous of creating food; *abhyatapat*, deliberated with regard to; *apaḥ*, the water, already mentioned. *Tābhyaḥ abhitaptābhyaḥ*, from the water that was brooded over, and that formed the material; *ajāyata*, evolved; *mūrtiḥ*, a solid form — which could provide support (for others) and which comprised the moving and the unmoving. *Yā vai sā mūrtiḥ ajāyata*, the form that evolved; *tat annam vai*, that formed thing is verily food.

तदेनत्सृष्टं पराङत्यजिघांसत्तद्वाचाऽजिघृक्षत् तन्नाशक्नोद्वाचा ग्रहीतुं। स यद्धैनद्वाचाऽग्रहैष्यदभिव्याहृत्य हैवान्नमत्रप्स्यत्॥३॥

3. This food, that was created, turned back and attempted to run away. He tried to take it up with speech. He did not succeed in taking it up through speech. If He had succeeded in taking it up with the speech, then one would have become contented merely by talking of food.

Tat enat annam, this aforesaid food; that was *sṛṣṭam*, created—in the presence of the senses and their deities. As a mouse, for instance, when in the presence of a cat, thinks, 'This is an eater of food and is Death to me', and moves back, similarly this food turned *parāk*, back; and *atyajighāṁsat*, wanted to go beyond the reach of the devourers; it began to run away. When that aggregate of the organs and their deities, that mass (Virāṭ) in the form of the body and senses (of Virāṭ), realized that intention of the food, but did not notice other eaters of food, He Himself being the first begotten, He *ajighṛkṣat*, tried to take up; *tat*, that food; *vācā*, through speech, through the act of speaking. *Na aśaknot*, He did not succeed; *grahītum tat*, to take up that; *vācā*, through speech, through speaking. *Yat*, if; *saḥ*, He, the First Born, the first embodied Being; *agrahaiṣyat*, had taken up; *enat*, this food; *vācā*, through speech; then everyone, being a product of the First Born; *atrapsyat*, would have become satisfied; *abhivyāhṛtya ha eva annam*, merely by talking of food. But, as a matter of fact, this is not the case. Hence we understand that the First

Born, too, did not succeed in grasping (food) through speech. The remaining portions are to be similarly explained.

तत्प्राणेनाजिघृक्षत् तन्नाशक्नोत्प्राणेन ग्रहीतुं स यद्धैनत्प्राणेनाग्रहैष्यदभिप्राण्य हैवान्नमत्रप्स्यत् ॥४॥

4. He tried to grasp that food with the sense of smell. He did not succeed in grasping it by smelling. If He had succeeded in grasping it by smelling, then everyone would have become contented merely by smelling food.

तच्चक्षुषाऽजिघृक्षत् तन्नाशक्नोच्चक्षुषा ग्रहीतुं स यद्धैनच्चक्षुषाऽग्रहैष्यद्दृष्ट्वा हैवान्नमत्रप्स्यत् ॥५॥

5. He wanted to take up the food with the eye. He did not succeed in taking it up with the eye. If He had taken it up with the eye, then everyone would have become satisfied by merely seeing food.

तच्छ्रोत्रेणाजिघृक्षत् तन्नाशक्नोच्छ्रोत्रेण ग्रहीतुं स यद्धैनच्छ्रोत्रेणाग्रहैष्यच्छ्रुत्वा हैवान्नमत्रप्स्यत् ॥६॥

6. He wanted to take up the food with the ear. He did not succeed in taking it up with the ear. If He had taken it up with the ear, then everyone would have become satisfied merely by hearing of food.

तत्त्वचाऽजिघृक्षत् तन्नाशक्नोत्त्वचा ग्रहीतुं स यद्धैनत्त्वचाऽग्रहैष्यत् स्पृष्ट्वा हैवान्नमत्रप्स्यत् ॥७॥

7. He wanted to take it up with the sense of touch. He did not succeed in taking it up with the sense of touch. If He had taken it up with touch, then everyone would have been satisfied merely by touching food.

तन्मनसाऽजिघृक्षत् तन्नाशक्नोन्मनसा ग्रहीतुं स यद्धैनन्म-
नसाऽग्रहैष्यद् ध्यात्वा हैवान्नगत्रप्स्यत् ॥८॥

8. He wanted to take it up with the mind. He did not succeed in taking it up with the mind. If He had taken it up with the mind, then everyone would have become satisfied by merely thinking of food.

तच्छिश्नेनाजिघृक्षत् तन्नाशक्नोच्छिश्नेन ग्रहीतुं स यद्धै-
नच्छिश्नेनाग्रहैष्यद्विसृज्य हैवान्नमत्रप्स्यत् ॥९॥

9. He wanted to take it up with the procreative organ. He did not succeed in taking it up with the procreative organ. If He had taken it up with the procreative organ, then everyone would have become satisfied by merely ejecting food.

तदपानेनाजिघृक्षत् तदावयत् सैषोऽन्नस्य ग्रहो यद्वायुरन्नायुर्वा
एष यद्वायुः ॥१०॥

10. He wanted to take it up with Apāna. He took it up. This is the devourer of food. That vital energy which is well known as dependent on food for its subsistence is this vital energy (called Apāna).

Being unable to take up the food through the nose, the

eye, the ear, the skin, the mind and the generative apparatus, that is to say, through the activity of the respective organs, at last He *ajighṛkṣat*, wanted to take up the food; *apānena*, by Apāna (the indrawing energy of) air—through the cavity of the mouth. *Tat āvayat*, (He) took up that food thus; He ate it. Therefore *saḥ eṣaḥ*, this Apāna air; *annasya grahaḥ*, (is) the seizer of food, i.e. the devourer of food. *Yat vāyuḥ* (should be rather *yaḥ vāyuḥ*), the vital energy that is; *annāyuḥ vai*, well known as dependent on food, for its subsistence; is *eṣaḥ*, this one; *yat vāyuḥ*, which is the vital energy, called Apāna.[1]

स ईक्षत कथं न्विदं मदृते स्यादिति स ईक्षत कतरेण प्रपद्या इति। स ईक्षत यदि वाचाऽभिव्याहृतं यदि प्राणेनाभिप्राणितं यदि चक्षुषा दृष्टं यदि श्रोत्रेण श्रुतं यदि त्वचा स्पृष्टं यदि मनसा ध्यातं यद्यपानेनाभ्यपानितं यदि शिश्नेन विसृष्टमथ कोऽहमिति ॥११॥

11. He thought, 'How indeed can it be there without Me?' He thought, 'Through which of the two ways should I enter?' He thought, 'If utterance is done by the organ of speech, smelling by the sense of smell, seeing by the eye, hearing by the ear, feeling by the sense of touch, thinking by the mind, the act of drawing in (or pressing down) by Apāna, ejecting by the procreative organ, then who (or what) am I?'

Having thus made the existence of the congress of the

[1] The eater of food is not the Self, but the vital energy that manifests itself as inhaling etc.

senses and their deities dependent on food, like the existence of a city, its citizens, and its rulers, *saḥ*, He; *īkṣata*, thought—like the ruler of the city, while cogitating thus: '*Katham nu*, how indeed; *mat-ṛte*, without Me, the master of the city; *syāt*, can there be; *idam*, this thing—this activity belonging to the body and the senses that will be spoken of—since it is meant for somebody else? *Yadi vācā abhivyāhṛtam*, if speaking is encompassed by the organ of speech, and so on, then use of speech etc. will become useless, will not take place in any way, just as offerings and praises that are made and sung by citizens and bards in honour of their lord become useless when the lord is not there. Therefore, just as a king is with regard to a city, so I should be there as the supreme lord, the ruler, the witness of whatever has been done or not done as also their results, and the enjoyer. It is a logical necessity that the combination of the products (i.e. the body and the organs) should be meant for somebody else. If this necessity can be fulfilled even without Myself—who am a conscious being and by whom enjoyment through them is sought for—just as much as the activities of a city and its citizens can be without their lord, *atha*, then; *kaḥ aham*, who or what, and whose lord am I? If, after entering into the combination of the body and the organs, I do not witness the fruits of utterances etc. made by speech etc., just as a king, after entering a city, observes the omissions and commissions of the officers, then nobody will understand or think of Me as, "This one is a reality and is of this kind." Contrariwise, I shall become cognizable as the conscious reality who knows as His objects such activities as utterance etc. of the organs of speech etc., and for whose sake exist these utterances etc. of such composite things as speech and so on, just as the pillars, walls, etc., that enter into the construction of a palace etc. exist for the sake of somebody else who (is sentient and) does not form a part of that structure.' Having reasoned thus, *saḥ*, He; *īkṣata*, thought; *iti*, thus; '*Katareṇa prapadyai*, through which shall I enter? There are two ways of entrance into this composite thing—the forepart of the foot and the head. *Katareṇa*, by which of these two paths; *prapadyai* (or rather, *prapadyeyam*), should I enter; into this city of the aggregate of body and organs?'

Having considered thus, 'That being so, I should not enter through the lower way—viz the two tips of the feet—that is the path of entry for My servant *Prāṇa* (the Vital Force), that is commissioned to act in every way on My behalf. What then (should I do)? As a last resort, let me enter by splitting up (the crown of) its head', (He entered) just like a human being who performs what he thinks.

स एतमेव सीमानं विदार्यैतया द्वारा प्रापद्यत। सैषा विदृतिर्नाम द्वास्तदेतन्नान्दनम्। तस्य त्रय आवसथास्त्रयः स्वप्ना अयमावसथोऽयमावसथोऽयमावसथ इति ॥१२॥

12. Having split up this very end, He entered through this door. This entrance is known as *vidṛti* (the cleft entrance). Hence it is delightful. Of Him there are three abodes—three (states of) dream. This one is an abode, this one is an abode, this one is an abode.

Saḥ, He, the Creator God; *etam eva sīmānam vidārya*, having cleft this very end, having made a hole at the farthest point where the hair is parted; *etayā dvārā*, through this gate, this entrance; *prāpadyata*, entered—into this world, i.e. into this conglomeration of body and organs. This one is that entrance that becomes well known from the fact of the perception inside (the mouth) of the taste etc. of oil and other things when these are applied on the crown of the head (for a long time). *Sā eṣā dvāḥ*, this door; *vidṛtiḥ nāma*, is well known as *vidṛti* (the cleft one), because of its having been cleft. As for the other entrances—viz the ear etc.—they are not rich, i.e. not sources of joy, since they are common passages meant for those occupying the places of servants etc. But this passage is only for the supreme Lord; *tat*, hence; *etat nāndanam*, this one is productive of joy. *Nāndana* is the same as *nandana*, the lengthening being a Vedic licence. It is so called because one revels (*nandati*) by going to the supreme Brahman through this door. *Tasya*, of Him, who, after having created thus, entered (the body) as an individual soul, like a king entering a city; there are *trayaḥ āvasathāḥ*, three abodes—viz the right eye, the seat of the sense (of vision), during the waking state; the mind inside, during the dream state; and the space within the heart, during the state of deep sleep. Or the three abodes may be the ones that will be enumerated, viz the body of the father, the womb of the mother, and one's own body. (He has) *trayaḥ svapnāḥ*, three (states of) dream, known as waking, dream, and deep sleep.

Objection: The waking state is not a dream, it being a state of consciousness.

Answer: Not so, it is verily a dream.

Objection: How?

Answer: Since there is no consciousness of one's own supreme Self, and in it are perceived unreal things as in a dream.

Ayam, this one—the right eye; is the first *āvasathaḥ*, abode; the second is the mind inside; and the space within the heart is the third. '*Ayam āvasathaḥ*, this is an abode' is only a recounting of what has been already enumerated. Residing alternately as identified with those abodes, this individual soul sleeps deeply for long through natural ignorance, and does not wake up, though experiencing the blows of sorrow which arise from the concurrence of many hundreds of thousands of calamities and which fall like the thumps of a heavy club.

स जातो भूतान्यभिव्यैख्यत् किमिहान्यं वावदिषदिति। स एतमेव पुरुषं ब्रह्म ततममपश्यत्। इदमदर्शमिती३ ॥१३॥

13. Being born, He manifested all the beings;[1] for did He speak of (or know) anything else?[2] He realized this very Puruṣa as Brahman, the most pervasive, thus: 'O! I have realized this.'

Saḥ jātaḥ, He being born, having entered into the body as the individual soul; *abhivyaikhyat*, manifested; *bhūtāni*, the beings. When, by good luck, a teacher of supreme compassion beat near his ears the drum of the great sayings of

[1] He knew and spoke distinctly of them as identified with Himself thus: 'I am a man', 'I am blind', 'I am happy', etc.

[2] That is to say, He neither perceived, nor spoke of anyone besides Himself. As He did not perceive any difference, He identified Himself with the individual soul.

the Upaniṣads whose notes were calculated to wake up the knowledge of the Self, then the individual *apaśyat*, realized; *etam eva*, this very; *puruṣam*, Puruṣa (as Brahman)—the Puruṣa that is being discussed as the Lord of creation etc., who is called Puruṣa because of residence (*śayana*, i.e. existence) in the city (*purī*) (of the heart). (He realized Him) as *brahma*, Brahman, the Great; which is *tatamam* (by adding the missing *ta*, and taking the form *tatatamam*, the word means) the most pervasive, the fullest, like space. How (did he realize)? '*Itī*, O!; I *adarśam*, have seen; *idam*, this one—this Brahman, that is the real nature of my Self.' The elongation (of *i* in *itī*) is in accordance with the rule that in the case of a word suggesting deliberation, the vowel gets lengthened.[1]

तस्मादिदन्द्रो नामेदन्द्रो ह वै नाम। तमिदन्द्रं सन्तमिन्द्र इत्याचक्षते परोक्षेण। परोक्षप्रिया इव हि देवाः। परोक्षप्रिया इव हि देवाः ॥१४॥

इत्यैतरेयोपनिषदि प्रथमाध्याये तृतीयः खण्डः ॥

14. Therefore His name is Idandra. He is verily known as Idandra. Although He is Idandra, they call Him indirectly Indra; for the gods are verily fond of indirect names, the gods are verily fond of indirect names.

Since He realized Brahman as 'this', i.e. directly—'the

[1] The elongation suggests that he first considered whether Brahman had been fully realized or not and then got the conviction, 'It is fully realized'. This conviction led to full satisfaction, expressed through the exclamation, 'O!'

Brahman that is immediate and direct, the Self that is within all' (Bṛ. III. iv. 1)—therefore, from the fact of seeing as '*idam*, this', the supreme Self is *idandraḥ nāma*, called Idandra. God is *idandraḥ ha vai nāma*, verily known as Idandra, in the world. *Tam idandram santam*, Him who is Idandra; they, the knowers of Brahman, *ācakṣate*, call; *parokṣeṇa*, indirectly, by an indirect name; *indraḥ iti*, as Indra. (They call Him thus) for the sake of conventional dealings, they being afraid of referring by a direct name, since He is the most adorable. So it follows that, *hi*, inasmuch as; *devāḥ*, the gods; are *parokṣapriyāḥ iva*, verily fond of the use of indirect names; it needs no mention that the great Lord, the God of all the gods, must be much more so. The repetition (in *parokṣapriyāḥ* etc.) is to indicate the end of the present Part (I).

PART II

CHAPTER I

Introduction: The purport of this Fourth[1] (i.e. the First) Part (just finished) is this: The Reality that is the creator, preserver, and destroyer of the universe, and is transcendental, omniscient, omnipotent, and all-knowing, created in due order this entire universe beginning with space, without the help of any substance other than Himself. Then He Himself entered into all the bodies possessed of vital force etc. for the sake of realizing His own Self. And having entered there, He realized directly His own Self in Its reality, as 'I am this Brahman'. Therefore He is the only one Self in all the bodies, and there is none besides. And so everybody else, too, should realize thus: 'He is my Self' (Kau. III. i. 8), 'I am Brahman' (Bṛ. I. iv 10).[2] Moreover, it has been said here, 'In the beginning this was but the absolute Self alone' (I. i. 1), and 'Brahman, the most pervasive' (I. iii. 13), and so also in other Upaniṣads.

Objection: For the One that is all-pervasive and that is the Self of all, there is not so much as the point of a hair unoccupied. Therefore how could He enter by splitting the end like an ant entering into a hole?

Answer: This is but an insignificant question to be posed when there are so many others that can be asked here.

[1] Fourth, counting from the First Part of the Āraṇyaka in which this Upaniṣad is included.

[2] In the Commentary the two texts seem to have become combined.

That without organs He thinks; without the help of anything He created this universe; gathering up (a lump of) the human size from water, He gave it shape; from His brooding parted the mouth etc., from which emerged Fire etc., the presiding deities of the organs; the deities became associated with hunger and thirst; they prayed for abodes; cows etc. were shown to them; they entered into their respective abodes; the created food ran away; there was an attempt at taking it up with the organ of speech etc.— all these are on a par with the (problem of) splitting the end and entering.

Objection: Then, let all of this, without exception, be incoherent.

Answer: No, there is no fault, since all this is but eulogistic,[1] the only thing sought to be taught here being the realization of the Self. Or a more reasonable explanation is that the Deity, who is omniscient and omnipotent and is a great conjurer, created all this like a magician; but the parable etc. are elaborated for the sake of easy instruction and comprehension just as it is done in ordinary life. For the mere acquaintance with anecdotes regarding creation etc. leads to no useful result, whereas it is well known in all the Upanisads that from the knowledge of the unity of the Self as Its real nature follows immortality as a result; and the same fact is in evidence in the Smṛtis like the *Gītā* in such sentences as '(He sees, who sees) the Lord Supreme, existing equally in all beings, (deathless in the dying)' (XIII. 27).

[1] *Arthavāda*: meant for emphasizing something other than the idea conveyed literally.

Objection: There are three souls: One is well known in the world and in all the scriptures as the transmigrating soul that enjoys and acts. The second soul is the omniscient God, the creator of the universe, the intelligent one. And He is inferable from the logical ground shown in the scriptures, viz the creation of bodies and worlds having many localities that are suitable for the enjoyment of the fruits of actions of innumerable beings, just as an architect etc. possessed of the requisite skill and knowledge can be inferred from the fact of the construction of a town, a palace, etc. The third is the all-pervading Consciousness (Puruṣa) presented by the Upanisads alone and well known from such texts as: 'From where speech turns back' (Tai. II. iv. 1), 'Not this, not this' (Bṛ. III. ix. 26). Thus there are these three selves distinct from one another. That being so, how can it be known that the Self is one without a second and transcendental?

Vedāntin: As to that, how is the individual soul even known?

Opponent: Is he not known as the hearer, thinker, seer, teacher, maker of (inarticulate) sounds, perceiver, and knower?

Vedāntin: Is it not contradictory to say of him, who is known through the act of hearing etc., that 'He thinks without being thought of, he knows without being known' (Bṛ. III. viii. 11, Ke. I. i. 6), and that 'You cannot think of that which is the thinker of thought; you cannot know that which is the knower of knowledge' (Bṛ. III. iv. 2) etc.?

Opponent: True, it will involve a contradiction if the individual soul is known directly like happiness etc. But as a fact, direct perception is denied by, 'You cannot think of that which is the thinker of thought', etc. But he is known through such inferential grounds as hearing etc. Hence how can there be a contradiction?

Vedāntin: How is he known even through such grounds of inference as hearing etc.? For when the Self is engaged in hearing an audible sound, it cannot have the actions of thinking and knowing with regard to Itself or anything else, since it is engrossed only in the act of hearing. So also with regard to other acts like thinking. And the acts of hearing etc. pertain to their own objects only (and not to their subjects); not that the act of thinking by the thinker can occur with regard to anything outside the thinkable.[1]

Opponent: Is not the mind able to think of everything?

Vedāntin: Truly this is so; still no thinkable can be thought of without the thinker.[2]

Opponent: Granted this is so, what follows?

Answer: This will be the accruing result here. He who is the thinker of all will simply be the thinker, and he will not be an object of thought. And there is not a second thinker who can think of that thinker. Should he be thinkable by the Self, then there will be the contingency (of the existence) of two Selves—the one being the Self by which the (thinking) Self is thought of and the other Self which is thought of. Or, the same Self will be split into two halves, like a bamboo, to become the thinker and the thinkable.

[1] The Self is not a thinkable object.

[2] Mind being only an instrument for the Self, an agent has to be posited to make the act of thinking possible.

But it is illogical either way. This is analogous to the case of two lamps which, because of their similarity, cannot be (mutually) the illuminator and the illumined. Besides, the thinker, while engaged in thinking of the thinkable object, has no time left out from the process of thinking during which to think of himself.[1] Even on the supposition that the thinker thinks of the Self through the grounds of inference, there will spring up two Selves—the one that is inferred through logical grounds, and the other that infers. Or the same Self will be split up. And so there will be the defect already mentioned.

Objection: If the Self be not known either through perception or inference, why is it said, 'One should realize thus: "He is my Self"' (Kau. III. 9)? Or why is the Self called the hearer, the thinker, etc.?

Answer: Is it not a fact that the Self is possessed of such qualities as the capacity of hearing;[2] and is it not well known (in the Upaniṣads) that It is free from such qualities as the capacity of hearing? What inconsistency do you find here?

Opponent: Though it may not strike you as incongruous, to me it is so.

Vedāntin: How?

Opponent: When the Self is a hearer, It is not a thinker; and when It is a thinker, It is not a hearer. That being so, It becomes a hearer and a thinker from one point of view, while from another It is neither a hearer nor a thinker. So

[1] The mind engages not in the Self but in things external to it.

[2] The Self is the eternal hearer, seer, etc.

with regard to other situations. That being so, how can you avoid the feeling of an irreconcilability in the face of the doubt that crops up as to whether the Self is possessed of the capacity to hear etc., or possessed of the opposite quality of not being able to hear etc.? At the time when Devadatta moves, he is not stationary, but is moving to be sure; and when he is motionless, he is not moving, but staying on. During such a period he can be either moving or staying as an only exclusive alternative; but he cannot be both moving and staying continuously. The same is the case here. Similar (also) is the view, in this matter, of the followers of Kaṇāda and others, according to whom the Self is called a hearer, a thinker, and so on because of Its being occasionally possessed of hearing etc. For they say that knowledge is a product of contact (between the mind and the senses), and that this contact is not simultaneous. And (as a proof) they adduce such illustrations as: 'My mind was occupied with some other object, so I did not see this.' And (they argue that) it is proper to accept the non-simultaneity of knowledge as a logical ground for inferring the existence of mind.[1] Let this be so. What do you lose if it be so?

Vedāntin: Let it be so if it be logical and if it pleases you. But it cannot be the meaning of the Upaniṣads.

Opponent: Is it not implied by the Upaniṣads that the Self is the hearer, thinker, etc.?

[1] If the mind did not exist, then all the senses, when simultaneously in contact with their objects, would preceive all the objects. But this is not a fact. So the Vaiśeṣikas believe in an atomic mind that gets connected with the senses in succession.

Vedāntin: No, since there is the statement that It is not the hearer, thinker, etc.[1]

Opponent: Was not that position denied by you by saying that It is occasionally so?

Vedāntin: No, for by me the Self is accepted as the eternal hearer etc., according to the Vedic text, 'For the listener's function of hearing can never be lost' etc. (Bṛ. IV. iii. 27).

Objection: If on that view hearing etc. are admitted as eternal, there will be the simultaneous origin of (all kinds of) knowledge, which will contradict experience. Besides, this will lead to the assumption of absence of ignorance in the Self. And that is unacceptable.

Answer: Neither of the defects arises, since according to the Upaniṣads, the Self can become the hearer etc. through Its (inherent) power of hearing etc.[2] (Bṛ. III. iv. 2). The seeing etc., by the impermanent and gross eyes etc. that are subject to conjunction and disjunction (with their objects), are impermanent indeed, just as the burning of fire is, because of its being produced from contact with hay etc. Not that the eternal and formless Self, which is free from the attributes of conjunction and disjunction, can have transitory qualities like seeing etc. that are caused by contact. In support of this is the Vedic text: 'The vision of the witness can never be lost' etc. (Bṛ. IV. iii. 23). From this it follows that there are two kinds of vision — the transitory vision of the eye and the eternal vision of the Self. Similarly,

[1] Seems to be a reference to Bṛ. IV. iv. 2.

[2] By virtue of Its being the witness of all mental changes involved in the acts of hearing etc.

there are two kinds of hearing—the transitory hearing of the ear and the eternal hearing of that which by nature is the Self. So also are there two kinds of thinking and two sorts of knowing—the external and the internal. For on this view alone, and only in the way it has been shown, does the Vedic text 'The seer of seeing and the hearer of hearing' (Bṛ. III. iv. 2) become justifiable. It is a matter of experience, too, that the vision of the eye is non-eternal, inasmuch as it is lost or regained in accordance as the disease called Timira sets in or is cured. Similar is the case with hearing and thinking. And the eternality of the vision etc. of the Self is well known in the world, for a man whose eyes have been plucked out says, 'My brother has been seen by me in dream today.' Similarly, a man who is known to be deaf may say, 'A *mantra* has been heard by me today in dream', etc. Should the eternal vision of the Self be produced merely through the contact of the eye, it should be destroyed on the destruction of the latter; and then a man whose eyes are plucked out should not perceive blue, yellow, etc. in dream. Moreover, such Vedic texts as, 'The vision of the witness can never be lost' etc. (Bṛ. IV. iii. 23), would be illogical; and the same will be the fate of such Vedic texts as, 'That is the eye in a man through which one sees in a dream.' The logical position is this: The eternal vision of the Self witnesses the ephemeral external vision; but since the external vision has such changing attributes as growth, decay, etc., the vision of the Self that witnesses it appears accordingly and seems to be ephemeral owing to the error of men. The case is similar to that of the vision fixed on a whirling firebrand or such other things, where the vision seems to be revolving (as the latter does). And in confirmation of this is the Vedic text, 'It thinks as it were, and shakes as it were' (Bṛ. IV. iii. 7). Hence the vision of the Self being eternal, it can have neither simultaneity, nor the opposite to it. But, for the ordinary people — owing to their preoccupation with the external limiting adjunct of ephemeral vision — and for the logicians, owing to their remaining outside scriptural tradition, it is quite possible to have the erroneous idea that the vision of the Self is impermanent.

The imagination of difference among God, the individual soul, and the supreme Self can also be traced to this very error; and equally erroneous it is to fancy such ideas as 'it is', 'it is not', with regard to the eternal and unconditioned vision of that Entity in which all the variations of speech and mind (i.e. name and form) get unified. He who entertains (with regard to that Reality beyond all speech and mind) any desire of fancying that It exists or does not exist; that It is one or is many; that It has attributes or has not; that It knows or does not; that It is active or is not; that It is fruitful or is fruitless; that It has a seed or is seedless; that It is happiness or is misery; that It is inside or is outside; that It is void or not; or that 'It is different (from me)', or that 'I am different (from It)'— (that man) may as well wish to roll up the sky like leather, to ascend there with his feet like ascending up a staircase, or to trace the footprints of the fish and birds in water and sky; for the Upaniṣadic texts declare: 'Not this, not this' (Bṛ. III. ix. 26), 'From which words turn back' (Tai. II. iv. 1), and so on. And there is the *mantra* text, 'Who indeed knows?' etc. (Ṛ. I. xxx. 6).

Objection: How then does he get the realization, 'He is

my Self'? Tell me, how can I realize Him as, 'He is my Self'.

Answer: Apropos of this, they relate a story: An idiotic person who committed some guilt was told, 'Fie on you! You are no man!' Because of his stupidity he approached somebody to get the conviction that he was a man and told him, 'Tell me who I am.' The latter understood his silliness and said, 'I shall make you understand by degrees.' And then after proving that he was not a motionless thing, and so on, he (the teacher) concluded with, 'You are none other than a man.' That dullard then told him, 'You who started to enlighten me have become silent. Why do you not instruct me?' That sentence of yours is just like this. How can he, who does not understand himself to be a man when told, 'You are none other than a man', understand himself to be a man even when told, 'You are a man'? Therefore the process to be followed in enlightening about the Self is as it is set forth in the scriptures and nothing else; for hay etc. that can be consumed by fire are not burnt by anything else. It is because of this that the scripture, which started to impart knowledge about the nature of the Self, stopped after declaring, 'Not this, not this' (Bṛ. III. ix. 26), just as it was done in the story after negating all that was other than man. And similar are the texts, 'Without interior or exterior' (Bṛ. II. v. 19, III. viii. 8), 'This Self, the perceiver of everything, is Brahman. This is the teaching' (Bṛ. II. v. 19), 'Thou art That' (Ch. VI. viii-xvi), 'But when to the knower of Brahman everything has become the Self, what should one see and through what?' (Bṛ. II. iv. 14, IV. v. 15); and there are still others.

As long as one does not realize thus this Self that has

been described, so long does one accept as one's Self the external limiting adjunct[1] which is in the form of ephemeral vision; and considering through ignorance the attributes of the limiting adjuncts as one's own, one transmigrates under the influence of ignorance, desire, and action, by rotating again and again through the regions of the gods, animals, and men, that range from Brahmā to a clump of grass. While transmigrating thus, one rejects the body assumed earlier, and giving it up, accepts another. In the course of showing what states one experiences as one continues thus without a break in the current of birth and death, as though in a river, the Upaniṣad says with a view to generating detachment:

ॐ पुरुषे ह वा अयमादितो गर्भो भवति यदेतद्रेतः। तदेतत्सर्वेभ्योऽङ्गेभ्यस्तेजः संभूतमात्मन्येवाऽऽत्मानं बिभर्ति तद्यदा स्त्रियां सिञ्चत्यथैनज्जनयति तदस्य प्रथमं जन्म ॥१॥

1. In man indeed is the soul first conceived. That which is this semen is extracted from all the limbs as their vigour. He holds that self of his in his own self. When he sheds it into his wife, then he procreates it. That is its first birth.

This very man performs such *karmas* as sacrifice etc. owing to his self-identification with ignorance, desire, and action; then he reaches the lunar region after passing from this world through smoke and the rest in succession; and then, when the fruits of his action become exhausted, he reaches this world to become food after passing in succession

[1] The mind whose vision is identical with itself and is external to the Self.

through rain etc.; then he is poured as a libation in the fire that is man. *Puruṣe ha vai*, in that man indeed; *ayam*, that, transmigrating soul; *āditaḥ garbhaḥ bhavati*, is first conceived, in the form of semen after passing through the (state of being the) essence of food etc. This is being stated by saying that he takes birth in that form, in the text, '*Yat etat retaḥ*.' *Taṭ etat retaḥ*, that which is this semen; *sambhūtam*, is accomplished, (extracted); as *tejaḥ*, vigour, essence, of the body; *sarvebhyaḥ aṅgebhyaḥ*, from all the limbs, from all the component parts, such as the juice of the body which is the product of food. Being identified with the man himself, this (semen) is called his self. He *bibharti*, bears; that *ātmānam*, self that has been conceived in the form of semen; *ātmani eva*, in his own self; (in other words) he holds his own self (the semen) in his own body. *Yadā*, when—when his wife is in the proper state; he *siñcati*, sheds, while in union; *tat*, that semen; *striyām*, in the wife—in the fire of the woman; *atha*, then; the father *janayati*, procreates; *enat*, this one—the semen that was conceived by him as identified with himself. *Asya*, of that transmigrating soul; *tat*, that, that issuing out of its own place, in the form of semen, when it is being poured out; is the *prathamam janma*, the first birth—the first manifested state. This fact was stated earlier by the text, 'This self (that is the man), (offers) this self of his (that is the semen), to that self of his (that is the wife).'

तत्स्त्रिया आत्मभूयं गच्छति यथा स्वमङ्गं तथा । तस्मादेनां न हिनस्ति । साऽस्यैतमात्मानमत्र गतं भावयति ॥२॥

2. That becomes non-different from the wife, just as much as her own limb is. Therefore (the foetus) does not

hurt her. She nourishes this self of his that has entered here (in her womb).

Tat, that, the semen; *gacchati*, becomes; *ātmabhūyam*, non-different—from the wife into whom it is shed; *yathā svam aṅgam tathā*, just like her own limb—her breast etc.—as it was in the case of the father. *Tasmāt*, because of this fact; the foetus *na hinasti*, does not hurt—like a boil; *enām*, this one—the mother. Since it has become a part of herself just like her breast etc., therefore it does not hurt her; this is the idea. *Sā*, she, that pregnant woman; understanding *etam ātmānam*, this self, of her husband; *atra gatam*, as having entered here—into her womb; *bhāvayati*, nourishes, protects it—by avoiding food etc. that are injurious to the foetus and by accepting such food etc. as are favourable to it.

सा भावयित्री भावयितव्या भवति। तं स्त्री गर्भं बिभर्ति। सोऽग्र एव कुमारं जन्मनोऽग्रेऽधिभावयति। स यत्कुमारं जन्मनोऽग्रेऽधिभावयत्यात्मानमेव तद्भावयत्येषां लोकानां सन्तत्या। एवं सन्तता हीमे लोकास्तदस्य द्वितीयं जन्म ॥३॥

3. She, the nourisher, becomes fit to be nourished. The wife bears that embryo (before the birth). He (the father) protects the son at the very start, soon after his birth. That he protects the son at the very beginning, just after birth, thereby he protects his own self for the sake of the continuance of these worlds. For thus is the continuance of these worlds ensured. That is his second birth.

Sā, she; the *bhāvayitrī*, nourisher, of the self of her husband, conceived in her womb; *bhāvayitavyā bhavati*, becomes fit to be nourished, to be protected, by the husband for, in this world, no one can have any relation with another unless it be through reciprocity of benefit. *Strī*, the wife; *bibharti*, bears; *tam garbham*, that foetus; *agre*, before its birth, by following the method of protecting the foetus mentioned earlier. *Saḥ*, he, the father; *bhāvayati*, protects, through natal rites etc.; *kumāram*, the son; *agre eva*, at the very start, as soon as he is born; *janmanaḥ adhi*, after the birth. *Yat*, that; *saḥ*, he, the father; *bhāvayati*, protects; *kumāram*, the son, through natal rites etc.; *agre janmanah adhi*, at the very start, just after the birth; *tat*, thereby; he *bhāvayati ātmānam eva*, protects his own self. For it is the father's self that takes birth as the son. And so has it been said, 'The husband enters into the wife' (Hari. III. lxxiii. 31). Now is being stated why the father protects after having begotten himself as the son: *eṣām lokānām santatyai*, for the continuance of these worlds. This is the idea. For these worlds will cease to continue if everyone should stop procreating sons etc. The idea is this: Since these worlds thus continue to flow like a current through the continuity of such acts as the begetting of sons, therefore these acts should be undertaken for the non-stoppage of the worlds, but not for the sake of emancipation. *Tat*, that fact, the issuing out; *asya*, of him, of the transmigrating soul, as a son from the mother's womb; is the *dvitīyam janma*, second birth, the manifestation of the second state, relatively to his form as semen.

सोऽस्यायमात्मा पुण्येभ्यः कर्मभ्यः प्रतिधीयते। अथास्याय-मितर आत्मा कृतकृत्यो वयोगतः प्रैति। स इतः प्रयन्नेव पुनर्जायते तदस्य तृतीयं जन्म ॥४॥

4. This self of his (viz the son) is deputed (by the father) for the performance of virtuous deeds. Then this other self of his (that is the father of the son), having got his duties fulfilled and having advanced in age, departs. As soon as he departs, he takes birth again. That is his third birth.

Sah ayam ātmā, that self which is the son; *asya*, of his, of the father; *pratidhīyate*, is deputed, by the father, in his own place; *puṇyebhyaḥ karmabhyaḥ*, for the performance of virtuous deeds, as prescribed by the scriptures, i.e. for the accomplishment of all that was the father's duty. Similarly it is seen in the Vājasaneyaka, in the portion dealing with the substitution (of the son), that on being instructed by the father, the son admits thus: 'I am Brahman (i.e. the Vedas), I am the sacrifice'[1] (Bṛ. I. v. 17). *Atha*, after that, after the father's responsibility has been entrusted to the son; *ayam itaraḥ ātmā*, this other self that is the father; *asya*, of this one, of the son; *kṛtakṛtyaḥ*, becoming freed from duties, from the three debts (to the gods, to the seers, and to the manes), i.e. having got all his duties fulfilled; *vayogataḥ*, having advanced in age, being afflicted with decrepitude; *praiti*, dies. *Saḥ itaḥ prayan eva*, as soon as he departs from here, no sooner does he leave the body than; he *punaḥ jāyate*, takes birth again, by adopting another body according to the results of his actions (by moving from one body to the other)

[1] The father's idea is this: 'Let the study of the Vedas (Brahman) which so long was my duty, devolve on you, for you are Brahman. Similarly, whatever sacrifices there are, that were to be performed by me, be henceforth performed by you, for you are the sacrifices.' All this the son accepts. (See Śaṅkara's commentary on the passage)

just like a leech. *Tat*, that, the birth that he gets after death; is *asya tṛtīyam janma*, the third birth of this one.

Objection: Is it not a fact that for the transmigrating soul the first birth is in the form of semen from the father? And his second birth has been stated to be as a son from the mother. The turn now being for stating the third birth of that very soul (which became the son), why is the birth of the dead father enumerated as the third?

Answer: That is not wrong, for the intention is to speak of the identity of the father and the son. That son, too, just like his father, entrusts his responsibility to his son (in his own turn) and then departing from here takes birth immediately after. The Upaniṣad thinks that this fact which is stated with regard to another (viz the father) is implied here (with regard to the son) also; for the father and the son are identical.

तदुक्तमृषिणा —
गर्भे नु सन्नन्वेषामवेद-
महं देवानां जनिमानि विश्वा
शतं मा पुर आयसीररक्ष-
न्नधः श्येनो जवसा निरदीयमिति ।
गर्भ एवैतच्छयानो वामदेव एवमुवाच ॥५॥

5. This fact was stated by the seer: 'Even while lying in the womb, I came to know of the birth of all the gods. A hundred iron citadels held me down. Then, like a hawk, I forced my way through by dint of the knowledge of the Self.' Vāmadeva said this while still lying in the mother's womb.

Transmigrating in this way, involved in the chain of birth and death through the manifestation of the three states, everyone remains merged in the ocean of this world. If he ever succeeds somehow, in any of the states, to realize the Self as revealed in the Vedas, he becomes freed then and there from all worldly bondages and accomplishes his object. The Upanisad says that *tat*, this fact; *uktam*, was declared; *ṛṣiṇā*, by the seer, by the (following) *mantra*, also; '*Garbhe nu san*, while still in the womb, of my mother —the indeclinable word *nu* implies deliberation; by virtue of the fruition of my meditations in many previous births, *aham*, I; *anvavedam*, knew, i.e. had the knowledge of; *viśvā janimāni*, all the births; *eṣām devānām*, of these gods—of Speech, Fire, etc. What a good luck! *Śatam*, a hundred, many; *āyasīḥ* (or rather *āyasyaḥ*) *puraḥ*, citadels made of iron, that is to say, impenetrable bodies as though made of iron; *arakṣan mā*, kept me guarded; *adhaḥ*, in the lower worlds; guarded me from getting freed from the meshes of the world. (Or *adhaḥ*, later on);[1] *śyenaḥ*, like a hawk; *javasā*, forcefully, through the power generated by the knowledge of the Self; *niradīyam*, I came out, by tearing through the net. O! the wonder!' *Vāmadevaḥ*, Vāmadeva, the seer; *garbhe eva śayānaḥ*, while still lying in the womb; *uvāca*, said; *etat*, this; *evam*, in this way.

स एवं विद्वानस्माच्छरीरभेदादूर्ध्व उत्क्रम्यामुष्मिन् स्वर्गे लोके सर्वान् कामानाप्त्वाऽमृतः समभवत् समभवत् ॥६॥

इत्यैतरेयोपनिषदि द्वितीयोऽध्यायः ॥

[1] Ānanda Giri gives these two alternative explanations of the word *adhaḥ* occuring in the commentary. There are two readings, *adho'dhaḥ* and *adho'tha*.

6. He who had known thus (had) become identified with the Supreme, and attained all desirable things (even here); and having (then) ascended higher up after the destruction of the body, he became immortal, in the world of the Self. He became immortal.

Saḥ, he, the seer Vāmadeva; *evam vidvān*, having known thus, known the Self as spoken of earlier; *asmāt śarīra-bhedāt*, after the destruction of this body—of this body that is conjured up by ignorance, that is impenetrable like iron; on the dissolution of the bondage of the bodies—subject to hundreds of multifarious evils consisting in birth, death, etc.—through the power generated by the tasting of the nectar of knowledge of the supreme Self; that is to say, on the destruction of the body following the destruction of such causes as ignorance that are the seeds of the creation of the body; he *ūrdhvaḥ* (*san*), having already become identified with the supreme Self; (then) *utkramya*, having ascended higher up as compared with the lowly worldly state, becoming established in the state of the pure, all-pervasive Self, shining with knowledge; *amusmin*, in that Reality, which was described as ageless, deathless, immortal, fearless, and omniscient, which has no cause or effect; inside or outside, which is of the nature of the unalloyed nectar of consciousness; he became merged like the blowing out of a lamp. He *samabhavat*, became; *amṛtaḥ*, immortal; *svarge loke*, in his own Self, in his own reality; *sarvān kāmān āptvā*, after the attainment of all desires; that is to say, after having got all the desirable things, even earlier (when still living), by virtue of his becoming desireless through the knowledge of the Self. The repetition in 'he became', is to show the end of the knowledge of the Self together with its fruit and its illustration.

PART III

CHAPTER I

There are Brāhmaṇas of modern times who crave for emancipation, hanker after the knowledge of Brahman, and realize that the achievement of identity with the Self of all follows from the disciplines for the knowledge of Brahman, as revealed by the Vedas through the succession of teachers like Vāmadeva and very well known in the councils of the knowers of Brahman. (These Brāhmaṇas) becoming desirous of desisting from the impermanent world of ends and means, inclusive of being born as limited souls, ask one another, thus, while engaged in deliberation: '*Kaḥ ayam ātmā*, which is this Self?' How do they ask?

ॐ कोऽयमात्मेति वयमुपास्महे कतरः स आत्मा। येन वा पश्यति येन वा शृणोति येन वा गन्धानाजिघ्रति येन वा वाचं व्याकरोति येन वा स्वादु चास्वादु च विजानाति ॥१॥

1. *Om*! Which is It that we worship as this Self? Which of the two is the Self? Is It that by which one sees, and by which one hears; also, by which one smells odour, and by which one utters speech, and by which one tastes the sweet or the sour?

The Self which *vayam upāsmahe*, we worship; directly *ayam ātmā iti*, as this Self; *kah*, which is It? And we worship that very Self, by meditating on which directly as 'This is the Self', Vāmadeva became immortal. Which indeed is that Self? When they were thus questioning one another with such eagerness to know, then from the impressions formed by having heard about the (two) specific entities dealt with earlier, there flashed in their minds the memory that here in the text, 'Brahman[1] entered into this person through the two ends of the feet', and 'Having split up this end, He entered through this door' (I.iii.12), have been mentioned two Brahmans which have entered into this very person from the opposite sides. And these two are the souls in this body. One of these selves is fit to be worshipped. While still engaged in discussion, they again asked one another with a view to determining clearly the Self that was to be worshipped out of the two. As they were discussing, there arose in them another thought regarding the one that should be the object of close enquiry. How? Two entities are perceived in this body: One is the instrument (Prāṇa), diversified into many forms, through which one perceives; and the other is the perceiver, inferable from the fact of the occurrence of recognition through memory of what was perceived with different senses.[2] Of these two, that through which one perceives cannot be the Self. Through what, again, does one perceive? That is being stated: *Yena vā paśyati*, is it that by which, transformed as eye, one sees colour; *yena vā*, that by vhich, transformed as the ear; *śṛṇoti*, one hears sound; *yena vā*, also, that by which, transformed as the sense of smell; *ājighrati gandhān*, one smells the odours; *yena vā*, and that by which, transformed as the organ of speech; one *vyākaroti vācam*, utters

[1] Prāṇa, the inferior Brahman, Hiranyagarbha.

[2] A man, with eyes plucked out, remembers the colour he had perceived before with his eyes. So also he thinks, 'I who saw before am hearing now.' This is impossible unless the perceiver is the same in the different situations.

speech, consisting of names, such as 'cow', 'horse', etc., and 'good', 'bad', etc.; *yena vā*, and that by which, transformed as the sense of taste; *vijānāti*, one perceives; *svādu ca asvādu ca*, the sweet and the sour (tastes).

Which, again, is that one organ that has become diversely differentiated? That is being answered:

यदेतद्धृदयं मनश्चैतत्। संज्ञानमाज्ञानं विज्ञानं प्रज्ञानं मेधा दृष्टिर्धृतिर्मतिर्मनीषा जूतिः स्मृतिः संकल्पः क्रतुरसुः कामो वश इति। सर्वाण्येवैतानि प्रज्ञानस्य नामधेयानि भवन्ति ॥२॥

2. It is this heart (intellect) and this mind that were stated earlier. It is sentience, rulership, secular knowledge, presence of mind, retentiveness, sense-perception, fortitude, thinking, genius, mental suffering, memory, ascertainment, resolution, life-activities, hankering, passion, and such others. All these verily are the names of Consciousness.

Etat, it is; *hṛdayam manaḥ ca*, the heart and the mind;[1] *yat*, that were spoken of earlier in 'The essence (i.e. the product) of all beings is the heart; the essence of the heart is the mind; by the mind was created water and Varuṇa; from the heart came the mind; and from the mind, Moon.' That very thing, which is but one, has become multiformed. Through this single internal organ, as transformed into the eye, one sees colour; through this, transformed

[1] The entity you asked about is the same as was referred to earlier as the heart (i.e. intellect), or the mind. This entity is the Prāṇa that assumes various aspects. It entered through the tip of the feet, whereas Brahman entered through the crown of the head.

into the ear, one hears; through this, transformed into the sense of smell, one smells; through this, transformed into the sense of taste, one tastes; through this very one, in its aspect as the organ of deliberation, one deliberates; and in its aspect as the heart (i.e. the intellect), one decides. Therefore this is the one single organ which acts with regard to all objects of the senses, so that the perceiver may perceive everything. Similar is the text of the Kauṣītakī Upaniṣad: 'Becoming identified with the organ of speech through the intellect (as reflecting the consciousness of the Self), the Self reaches (i.e. becomes identified with) the names[1] etc.' (III. 6). And in the Vājasaneyaka occur these: 'It is through the mind that one hears' (Bṛ. I. v. 3), 'for one knows colours through the heart' (Bṛ. III. ix. 19), etc. Accordingly, the entity that is called the heart and the mind is well known as the agent producing all perceptions. And the Prāṇa consists of these two, for there occurs the *brāhmaṇa* text: 'That which is the Prāṇa is the intellect; that which is the intellect is the Prāṇa' (Kau. III. 3). And we said in the texts dealing with the conversations with the Prāṇa and so on (Bṛ. I. iii, VI. i. 7–14; Pr. II) that the Prāṇa is of the form of a combination of the organs. Therefore the entity, (in the form of which) Brahman entered through the feet, cannot be the Self to be worshipped, since it is a subsidiary thing, being an instrument of perception for the perceiver. As a last resort, they arrived at this certitude: 'That witnessing Self is worthy of worship by us, for whose percep-

[1] The intellect becomes transformed into the organ of speech, and speech into words. The Self, too, through superimposed self-identification, seems to assume those forms, though It still remains as their illuminator.

tion the functions of this instrument, in its aspects as the heart and the mind, are being stated.'

The functions of that inner organ—with regard to internal and external objects—which take place for bearing witness to the witnessing Brahman[1] that is consciousness by nature and that exists in the midst of Its limiting adjunct, viz the internal organ, are (these that are) being enumerated: *Saṁjñānam*, sentience, the state of consciousness; *ājñānam*, rulership, the state of lordliness; *vijñānam*, (secular) knowledge of arts etc.; *prajñānam*, presence of mind; *medhā*, ability to understand and retain the purport of books; *dṛṣṭiḥ*, perception, of all objects through the senses; *dhṛtiḥ*, fortitude, by which the drooping body and senses are buoyed up—for they say, 'By fortitude they buoyed up the body'; *matiḥ*, thinking; *manīṣā*, independent thinking (genius); *jūtiḥ*, mental suffering, owing to disease etc.; *smṛtiḥ*, memory; *saṁkalpaḥ*, ascertainment, of colours etc. as white, black, etc.; *kratuḥ*, resolution; *asuḥ*, any function calculated to sustain life's activity, such as breathing etc.; *kāmaḥ*, desire for a remote object, hankering; *vaśaḥ*, passion for the company of women; *iti*, etc., and other functions of the inner organ. Since these are the means for the perception of the witness who is mere Consciousness, they are the limiting adjuncts of Brahman that is pure Consciousness, and therefore *saṁjñāna* etc. become the indirect names of Brahman, created by limiting adjuncts. *Sarvāṇi eva etāni*, all these verily; *bhavanti*, become; *nāmadheyāni*, the names; *prajñānasya*, of Consciousness; but not so

[1] Brahman cannot be perceived since It is not an object of cognition, and It is attributeless. Still, without being objectified, It is perceivable as the witness of mental states—A.G.

naturally and directly. And so has it been said, 'When It does the function of living, It is called the vital force' (Bṛ. I. iv. 7) etc.

एष ब्रह्मैष इन्द्र एष प्रजापतिरेते सर्वे देवा इमानि च पञ्च महाभूतानि पृथिवी वायुराकाश आपो ज्योतींषीत्येतानीमानि च क्षुद्रमिश्राणीव। बीजानीतराणि चेतराणि चाण्डजानि च जारुजानि च स्वेदजानि च चोद्भिज्जानि चाश्वा गावः पुरुषा हस्तिनो यत्किंचेदं प्राणि जङ्गमं च पतत्रि च यच्च स्थावरं सर्वं तत्प्रज्ञानेत्रम् प्रज्ञाने प्रतिष्ठितं प्रज्ञानेत्रो लोकः प्रज्ञा प्रतिष्ठा प्रज्ञानं ब्रह्म ॥३॥

3. This One is (the inferior) Brahman; this is Indra, this is Prajāpati; this is all these gods; and this is these five elements, viz earth, air, space, water, fire; and this is all these (big creatures), together with the tiny ones, that are the procreators of others and referable in pairs—to wit, those that are born of eggs, of wombs, of moisture, and of the earth, viz horses, cattle, men, elephants, and all the creatures that there are which move or fly and those which do not move. All these are impelled by Consciousness; all these have Consciousness as the giver of their reality; the universe has Consciousness as its eye, and Consciousness is its end. Consciousness is Brahman.

Eṣah, this One, the Self, which is essentially Consciousness; is *brahma*, Brahman, the inferior one (who is Hiraṇyagarbha and) who as Prāṇa (possessed of the power of action) and the conscious soul (possessed of the power of knowledge) exists in (the sum total of) all the bodies (i.e.

in the cosmic gross body) after having entered into all the limiting adjuncts of the internal organs (i.e. into the cosmic subtle body) like the reflection of the sun on diverse waters. He is the power of action and knowledge (in the individual). *Eṣaḥ*, this One; is verily *indraḥ*, Indra, who is called so because He possesses the qualities (mentioned earlier in I. iii. 13-14); or 'Indra' means the lord of the gods. *Eṣaḥ*, this One; is *prajāpatiḥ*, Prajāpati (Virāṭ) who is the first embodied Being[1]. That Prajāpati, from whom the presiding deities of the organs, viz Fire and others, were born after the formation of the cavity of the mouth etc., is verily this One. And *ete sarve devāḥ*, all these gods, viz Fire and others, that there are, are but this One; *ca*, and; *imāni pañca mahābhūtāni*, these five great elements; viz *etāni*, these—starting with earth—which are the materials of all the bodies and which constitute the foods and the eaters; besides, *ca imāni*, these also, e.g. snakes etc.; *ksudramiśrāni iva*, together with the tiny creatures—the word *iva* being meaningless; and which are *bījāni*, the seeds, causes (of others); *ca itarāṇi itarāṇi*, as well as those others and others, that are mentionable in pairs (e.g. the moving and the stationary). Which are they? They are being enumerated: *aṇḍajāni*, born of eggs—birds and others; *jārujāni*, born of wombs—men and others; *svedajāni*, born of moisture—lice etc.; and *udbhijjāni*, born of earth—e.g. trees etc.; *aśvāḥ*, horses; *gāvaḥ*, cattle; *puruṣāḥ*, human beings; *hastinaḥ*, elephants; *yat kim ca idam*, and whatever living creature there may be. Which are they? Whichever is *jaṅgamam*, moving on feet; and whichever is

[1] Hiraṇyagarbha identifies Himself with the cosmic subtle body, but Virāṭ with the cosmic gross body.

patatri, flying in the sky; and whatever is *sthāvaram*, motionless—all that is but this One. *Tat sarvam*, all that, without exception; is *prajñānetram*, made to exist by Consciousness—(the phrase being derived thus): *Prajñā* is Consciousness that is the same as Brahman; *netra* is that by which one is dowered with substance, or that by which one is impelled (to one's natural activity); therefore that which has Consciousness as the giver of its substance or as its impeller is *prajñānetram*. *Prajñāne pratiṣṭhitam*, on Consciousness it is established, that is to say, it is supported by Brahman during creation, existence, and dissolution. The sentence, '*prajñānetraḥ lokaḥ*, the universe has Consciousness as its impeller', is to be understood as before; or the meaning is that all the universe has got consciousness as its *netra*, eye (i.e. the source of revelation). *Prajñā*, Consciousness; is *pratiṣṭhā*, the support, of the whole universe.[1] Therefore *prajñānam brahma*, Consciousness is Brahman.

That Entity, thus dealt with, when freed from all distinctions created by the limiting adjuncts, is without stain, without taint, without action, quiescent, one without a second, to be known as 'Not this, not this' (Br. III. ix. 26), by the elimination of all attributes, and (It is) beyond all words and thoughts. That very Entity, which is the omniscient God—because of the association with the limiting adjunct of very pure intelligence—and is the ordainer of the common seed of all the unmanifested universense,

[1] Consciousness is self-revealing and is not dependent on any other factor for the revelation of Itself or of others. Or the sentence may mean that Consciousness is the one reality in which all phenomenal things end, just as the superimposed snake etc. end in their bases, the rope etc., after the dawn of knowledge.

assumes the name of *antaryāmī* (the Inner Controller) by virtue of being the Guide. That Entity Itself assumes the name of Hiraṇyagarbha, who identifies Himself with (cosmic) intelligence which is the seed of the manifested world. That Entity Itself gets the name of Virāṭ, Prajāpati, who has as His limiting adjunct the (gross, cosmic) body born first within the cosmic egg; and It comes to be known as the deities, Fire, etc., by assuming their (respective) limiting adjuncts (viz speech etc.) born from that egg. Similarly, Brahman gets the respective names and forms as conditioned by the divergent bodies, ranging from that of Brahmā to that of a clump of grass. It is the same Entity that has become diversified according to the variety of the limiting adjuncts and is known in every way and is thought of multifariously by all creatures as well as the logicians. And there are the Smṛti texts, 'Some call this very Entity Fire, some call It Manu, and some Prajāpati. Some call It Indra, while others call It Prāṇa and still others, the eternal Brahman', etc. (M. XII. 123).

स एतेन प्रज्ञेनाऽऽत्मनाऽस्माल्लोकादुत्क्रम्यामुष्मिन्स्वर्गे लोके सर्वान् कामानाप्त्वाऽमृतः समभवत् समभवत् ॥४॥

इत्यैतरेयोपनिषदि तृतीयोऽध्यायः ॥

4. Through this Self that is Consciousness, he ascended higher up from this world, and getting all desires fulfilled in that heavenly world, he became immortal, he became immortal.

Saḥ, he, Vāmadeva, or somebody else, knew thus the Brahman as described, through the Self that is Consciousness—through that very conscious Self by which the seers of old became immortal. Similarly, this enlightened one, too, *etena prajñena ātmanā*, through (i.e. in identification with) this (very) Self that is Consciousness; *asmāt lokāt utkramya*, ascending higher up from this world—the portion starting from here was explained before (II. i. 6). Ascending higher up from this world and *sarvān kāmān āptvā*, attaining all the desires; *amuṣmin svarge loke*, in that heavenly world; (he) *samabhavat*, became; *amṛtaḥ*, immortal; *samabhavat*, (he) became (immortal). *Om*.

ॐ वाङ् मे मनसि प्रतिष्ठिता मनो मे वाचि प्रतिष्ठित-माविरावीर्म एधि वेदस्य म आणीस्थः श्रुतं मे मा प्रहासीरनेना-धीतेनाहोरात्रान् संदधाम्यृतं वदिष्यामि सत्यं वदिष्यामि तन्मा-मवतु तद्वक्तारमवत्ववतु मामवतु वक्तारमवतु वक्तारम् ॥

ॐ शान्तिः शान्तिः शान्तिः ॥

INDEX TO THE TEXT